Doing Civility

Doing
Civility

Breaking the Cycle
of Incivility on the Campus

Kent M. Weeks

NEW YORK

Doing Civility
Breaking the Cycle of Incivility on the Campus

© 2014 **Kent M. Weeks.**

Published in New York, New York, by Morgan James Publishing. Morgan James and The Entrepreneurial Publisher are trademarks of Morgan James, LLC. www.MorganJamesPublishing.com

The Morgan James Speakers Group can bring authors to your live event. For more information or to book an event visit The Morgan James Speakers Group at www.TheMorganJamesSpeakersGroup.com.

FREE eBook edition for your existing eReader with purchase

PRINT NAME ABOVE

For more information, instructions, restrictions, and to register your copy, go to www.bitlit.ca/readers/register or use your QR Reader to scan the barcode:

ISBN 978-1-63047-070-8 paperback
ISBN 978-1-63047-071-5 eBook
ISBN 978-1-63047-072-2 hardcover
Library of Congress Control Number:
2013957725

Cover Design by:
Todd Engel, Engel Creative, Inc.
http://www.toddengel-engelcreative.com

Interior Design by:
Bonnie Bushman
bonnie@caboodlegraphics.com

In an effort to support local communities, raise awareness and funds, Morgan James Publishing donates a percentage of all book sales for the life of each book to Habitat for Humanity Peninsula and Greater Williamsburg.

Get involved today, visit
www.MorganJamesBuilds.com

Habitat
for Humanity®
Peninsula and
Greater Williamsburg
Building Partner

Table of Contents

Acknowledgments

I have been interested in the topic of civility for a long time. As a political scientist, lawyer, and teacher I have worked with colleagues and students on solving problems and developing policies to address the issues of the day. But reforming the structures of the university or the government can only do so much to mediate the conflicting passions of the moment. Only individuals, sometimes acting in a collective capacity, can do that. The question for me has been how can colleges help to shape our future leaders who will act and lead with civility and inspire others to do the same.

Following the publication of *In Search of Civility: Confronting Incivility on the College Campus* in 2011, I spoke with members of college communities across the country. Students were really interested in improving the climate of civility on their campuses, as were their professors and college leaders. Many of them expressed dismay about the uncivil behavior they observe in the media and in public discourse. In my discussions on campuses I heard many examples of ways in which colleges were trying to channel youthful energy to nurture a caring community. The questions that grew of out the discussions prompted new topics to explore.

The current book, *Doing Civility: Breaking the Cycle of Incivility*, is an outgrowth of these discussions and a companion book to *In Search of Civility*. Ernie Gilkes, my paralegal and law student, was instrumental in researching and writing the book. Sandy Crain and MacKenzie Grant provided valuable editorial assistance. My wife, Karen, read several drafts and offered ideas along the way. I am deeply grateful for their collective contributions.

Introduction

Civility—or more appropriately the lack of civility—is a topic that has drawn considerable attention recently. If the latest polls and surveys are any indication, there is broad consensus that incivility is a significant problem in the United States. In our complex, fast-paced, and constantly changing world, perhaps we have become more calloused and cynical in regard to the people around us. Frankly, it is increasingly difficult not to be a little cynical.

We constantly live with threats of terrorism, random mass-shootings, economic uncertainty, political polarization, and global unrest. Too many leaders and role models in politics, business, sports, and education project an image that is less than civil. Success is so often equated with doing whatever it takes to get to the top. This may require using other people, bending the rules, or engaging in conduct that is unethical or even illegal. It is no longer surprising when trusted people and organizations lie, cheat, and steal. The spiraling chaos that often surrounds us certainly contributes to the waning of civility in our culture.

The discussion of civility is particularly important for students on college and university campuses. The modern university may offer the best and most effective forum for providing an education in civility for our future leaders. Students currently entering their college years have a high degree of awareness of problems in their world and feel obligated to contribute to solving them. Perhaps the greatest chance of breaking the cycle of incivility that continues to escalate in our society is to educate students about the value of civil engagement. Students who understand the importance of civility and are given practical opportunities to serve are more likely to continue civil engagement when they enter the workplace or take positions of leadership.

While identifying the problem is a good first step, the next logical step is to determine what we can do to improve our incivility. The starting point is to have a concise understanding of what civility is and what civility is not. Within the context of this book, civility has two overarching characteristics—it requires mutual respect to be extended to others and an individual commitment to engage and strengthen the community. Using the dual principles of mutual respect and community engagement, the book vividly illustrates how incivility in politics, popular culture, education, and the workplace can negatively affect students and the community. However, the analysis does not end there. The book attempts to demonstrate an alternate way to approach civility dilemmas and do civility.

Taking meaningful steps to address incivility is critical to the future of our nation. As we become an increasingly diverse country, we must have citizens who are able to work together for the common good on complicated and complex issues. However, the challenge is figuring out how to tame the current environment of incivility that is growing deep cultural roots. When one looks behind the data and statistics on incivility, the truth is that many extraordinary people in our communities are doing civility and doing it well.

More often than not, when it really matters, people can do the right thing. In times of crises, tragedies, and disasters, Americans have proven their ability to look past difference and serve in extraordinary ways. Clearly, we know how to behave. But tapping in to this internal reservoir of civility requires a different mind-set. It requires extending mutual respect to others and treating them with dignity despite differences. It requires service and commitment to the community to make it stronger and better for everyone.

To facilitate our discussion on doing civility, we will follow four college students—Lindsey, Sonam, Antonio, and Jacob—and other students as they encounter civility dilemmas. These four students first appeared in the book *In Search of Civility: Confronting Incivility on the College Campus.* They are back to help provide the setting in which we can more clearly identify what civility and incivility look like in practice. The students are older and perhaps a little wiser; however, the real-life problems they encounter challenge them in new and deeper ways to reflect on their conduct, values, and beliefs.

This book is a companion publication to *In Search of Civility: Confronting Incivility on the College Campus.* By reading both books, readers have a vivid context for understanding civility and applying it in their everyday lives.

This book addresses some of the main places where we encounter incivility in our society, including political life, popular culture, higher education, and the workplace. We must work with those who desire to engage in civility. Real-life examples demonstrate civility that is both countercultural and inspiring.

Each chapter concludes with practical tools and exercises to help readers engage more fully with the reading and to challenge them to be more open, respectful, and community conscious. These tools include quizzes, role-playing exercises, vignettes, and other resources that will help readers do civility. We encourage groups using the book to take advantage of these tools for participating in small-group activities.

Every action done in company ought to be with some sign of respect to those that are present.
—George Washington
110 Rules of Civility and Decent Behavior

CHAPTER 1

Doing Civility

C hances are if you asked a random person on the street whether incivility was a problem, you would get a resounding "Yes!" Most Americans believe our society has become more rude and uncivil. A recent Pew Civility in America poll found that 63 percent of Americans believe that we have a civility problem, and 55 percent expect incivility to get worse.[1]

Although there appears to be general consensus that we have a civility problem, just what do we mean by civility? Civility is typically associated with good manners, for example, saying "please" and "thank you," or doing an act of courtesy, such as holding a door open for a mother pushing a stroller. Others associate civility with proper etiquette, such as table manners or decorum—for example, referring to an authority figure as "sir" or "ma'am" out of deference and respect. The understanding of civility as politeness is consistent with common definitions found in most dictionaries.[2]

1

While good manners, courtesy, and etiquette are important, our perceived civility problem is more than just a niceness deficiency or the consumption of a salad with the wrong fork.

Over the years, researchers, commentators, and civility-based organizations have grappled with trying to define fully the concept of civility. There is agreement that civility unequivocally includes politeness, perhaps as a starting point, but the concept is much deeper. P. M. Forni, cofounder of the Johns Hopkins Civility Project and an early leader in the modern civility movement, defines *civility* in part as a "form of goodness" that entails an "attitude of benevolent and thoughtful relating to other individuals" and "an active interest in the well-being of our communities."[3] Stephen Carter, a Yale law professor and author, defines *civility* as "an attitude of respect, even love, for our fellow citizens."[4]

The political nonprofit Institute for Civility in Governance defines *civility* as being "characterized by true respect for others."[5] The definition explains that *civility* "is about constantly being open to hear, to learn, to teach and to change" and "seeks common ground as a beginning point for dialogue."[6] Although not offering a specific definition, the National Institute for Civil Discourse, chaired by former U.S. presidents George H. W. Bush and Bill Clinton, explains *civility* as "respect for difference and willingness to compromise, most importantly for the good of generations of Americans to come."[7]

These more expansive definitions draw on certain common elements—politeness, mutual respect, and citizenship. Each element is individually distinctive. Yet when considered together in the context of civility, they coalesce around the common theme of genuinely recognizing the value and worth of a diverse people with varied ideas. A civil person chooses to extend politeness and mutual respect—even when there are significant differences in values and beliefs. Likewise, a civil person chooses to become an engaged citizen, not to dominate but to ensure the betterment of the community.

The politeness and mutual respect elements embedded in the broader definition of civility are reminiscent of a basic religious concept that is ancient and timeless: the Golden Rule. According to the Golden Rule,

"You shall love your neighbor as yourself."[8] In other words, as long as people act with general regard for their neighbors and treat them with the same degree of respect and care that they would wish to be treated, they have fulfilled the requirement of the Golden Rule. Thus civility is measured and assessed based on our desire to be treated with dignity and respect. Viewing civil conduct as an extension of the Golden Rule may seem rudimentary, yet the application is profound. What if more politicians addressed their policy differences based on the Golden Rule? What if more employers managed their employees on the basis of mutual respect? What if doctors, lawyers, accountants, teachers, and other service professionals adopted a Golden Rule approach to their occupations?

The citizenship element of civility is consistent with the etymology of the word itself. The modern English word *civility* comes from the Latin word *civitas*, meaning "city," in the sense of civic community.[9] So in some sense, civility incorporates a notion that includes a personal responsibility to a community. An example of the *civitas* concept is the ancient oath that Athenian citizens took to leave their city "not diminished, but better and better than before" to future generations.[10] Today, this sense of civility might manifest in an individual's choice to contribute to the community through volunteer organizations, civic institutions, or public service. All of these behaviors demonstrate a concern not only for oneself but also for the community in which one lives.

By combining the Golden Rule with the idea that civility carries with it the obligation to a civic community writ large, we have a concrete notion of civility that can inform the rest of our discussion. Distilled to its essence, civility is a combination of considerate conduct toward others embodied in the Golden Rule and a notion of civic duty and responsibility to the community.

CULTURE OF INCIVILITY

Incivility is commonplace in our culture. The new norm has been to expect some level of rudeness and disrespect in just about every facet of our lives. People drive recklessly and without regard to others on the road. Many engage in loud and obnoxious cell phone conversations in restaurants, on buses, or even in movie theaters. Others deliberately litter, dropping trash in the streets and public areas such as parks. Rude and unprofessional behavior is pervasive in almost every sector of business.

The poster children for incivility in America are politicians. Our political leaders have become ineffective because they cannot reach meaningful consensus on important issues like tax reform, immigration, and deficit reduction. Instead of collaborating to find solutions, battling factions adopt a my-way-or-the-highway approach to problem solving. Competing political parties attempt to legislate by energizing their bases and vilifying the opposition with insults and inflammatory rhetoric. The party that makes the most noise wins. This inability of our political leaders to constructively work together has created deep-rooted schisms throughout our society. *E Pluribus Unum*—the Latin phrase meaning "one from many" that is inscribed on the Great Seal of the United States—is losing its significance as we continue to allow our diversity to separate us into homogenous boxes.[11]

Incivility is not limited to politics, of course. It seems to be pervasive throughout many sectors of our society. Shocking uncivil conduct among business executives, performing artists, athletes, and Hollywood celebrities seems to capture the attention of both the media and the public. Indeed, we've reached a point where incivility isn't just unremarkable[12]—it's considered marketable and entertaining. The more shocking the story, the more it captivates our attention.

Also complicating matters is our technology addiction. Our eyes are constantly glued to mobile devices—sending texts, updating our status, downloading apps. Ear buds drown out the ambient noise of the people around us, and we fill our heads with MP3s, podcasts, and Internet radio, where we can completely control the content. Mature video games, with lifelike high-definition graphics, create virtual worlds where players—often children—are flooded with intense images of violence, blood and gore, and sexual content.[13] We are increasingly connected to technology but disconnected from each other.

In our fast-paced, overextended, and often self-absorbed lives, noticing the needs of others is difficult. Like the proverbial frog that slowly cooks in the warming kettle of cold water, the intensity of incivility begins to reach a boil, while we remain oblivious to the ensuing danger.

The growing culture of incivility is critically important because it represents a lack of consideration for others. Left unchecked, this lack of respect can escalate to even more dangerous forms of uncivil conduct. Consider the string of Columbine-style shootings that have occurred in high schools, colleges, and shopping malls over the last decade, culminating in the latest tragedy at Sandy Hook Elementary School in Newtown, Connecticut, where a deranged man opened fire in the school, killing six adults and twenty children.[14]

DEFINING CIVILITY

So what does civility look like in practice? This is perhaps the easier question to answer. Civility usually is demonstrated through manners, courtesy, politeness, and a general awareness of the rights, wishes, concerns, and feelings of others. Showing deference to others, particularly those in authority, is another example of civil conduct. Civility can also be seen when we are willing to embrace diversity and respect individuals with differing backgrounds, values, and beliefs. Making a point to listen to others and respond to the actual meanings they are trying to communicate—whether or not they are expressly articulated in words—is another example of civility.[15] Being mindful of the sensitivities of those with whom we speak and adjusting our speech and conduct accordingly also demonstrate civility.[16] In this sense, civility is simply a form of personal conduct that shows respect and appreciation for others.

Civility is more than just manners, politeness, and respect, however. The *civitas* side of civility calls for us to give of ourselves to strengthen the community, usually at the sacrifice of our wishes and desires. In this sense, serving with a volunteer organization for the purpose of aiding others in the community is a form of civility. Likewise, running for public office—assuming that there are no ulterior selfish motives involved—is a display of civility. We can think of it this way: while manners focus on the exchanges between and among individuals, civility also includes the exchange between an individual and the community. Good manners and polite interactions with others foster a sense of community that strengthens the community as a whole.

Incivility can be manifested in many ways. Conduct such as driving while intoxicated, cheating, plagiarizing, discriminating, and bullying are examples of uncivil behavior. Such conduct does not take into consideration the needs of others and may weaken or compromise the cohesiveness of a community. Incivility may also manifest itself in the workplace. From overbearing supervisors and contentious coworkers to hostile clients and customers, incivility is persistent in the workplace.[17] Again, an uncivil workplace is devoid of mutual respect for other employees and creates an environment that is hostile, fragmented, and unproductive.

CIVILITY DOES NOT . . .

Civility does not require neutrality. We can still espouse strong views that may be contrary to others. The key is to realize that there are many diverse people, ideas, and beliefs. While we may not agree with everyone, civility requires that we extend mutual respect—a notion that is easier said than done.

Civility is not the absence of conflict. In a democratic society dissent is healthy. Sometimes dissenters rock the boat and cause conflict, yet such conflict need not be uncivil. Consider Mohandas Gandhi's "Salt March" that defied the British monopoly on salt production,[18] Rosa Parks's refusal to give up her seat on the racially segregated bus,[19] or the many brave women, such as Susan B. Anthony and Inez Milholland, who marched, protested, and lobbied for the right to vote during the women's suffrage movement.[20] These social and political innovators sparked revolutions through meaningful dissent. Although they might have broken civil laws, the conflicts were intended to bring awareness to issues and advocate for change, not to attack people who held opposing views.

Clearly, there can be civil dissent without uncivil vitriolic personal attacks. However, the line between opposing an issue and opposing an individual can be razor thin. The contention created by hot button issues such as gay marriage, abortion, and gun control often involves deep-rooted cultural, political, and philosophical differences. Challenging a position in these issues can easily slide into personal attacks. Yet in a civilized and increasingly diverse democratic society, we must aspire to find ways to respect our differences and work toward the betterment of the entire community. Although we are different, we all share common values that are universal—love, honesty, fairness, freedom, and mutual respect.[21]

Civility does not conflict with the concept of freedom of speech or expression. Many critics regard civility policies as a backdoor way to restrict speech. Over the years, students and civil liberties groups have challenged the constitutionality of civility policies. However, civility should not be thought of as a legalistic code that establishes strict conduct guidelines. Instead, civility promotes and enhances free speech. When people are able to engage in dialogue from a position of mutual respect, the outcome is likely to be more productive than the abrasive shouting matches that have been misconstrued as free speech. The emphasis on civility in public discourse should not constrain speech or expression; rather it should enhance its efficacy and encourage respectful engagement.

LESS TALK, MORE ACTION

Even though there are obvious civility problems in our society, all is not lost. The fact that we are admitting we have a civility problem is the first step toward making positive change. A civility movement has emerged across many sectors of our society as a growing number of people are dissatisfied with the status quo. Researchers continue to study incivility and its effect in politics, culture, education, and the workplace. The general consensus is that our lack of civility is hurting us. The challenge is figuring this out: How do you do civility?

This book seeks to find constructive ways to apply the concept of civility to our everyday lives. Simply recognizing incivility is not enough. However, doing civility is complex—especially when we have become accustomed to incivility. Not everyone is going to play by the same code of conduct. There is a very good chance that the civility we extend will not be reciprocated by others. To effectuate change, someone must be willing to have the courage to break the cycle.

TOOLS AND EXERCISES

Civility: True or False?

Answer the following statements as being either "True" or "False," and explain your answer. Draw on your personal experience when answering. There is no right or wrong answer, but answer each statement honestly.

It would be *civil* to:

1. Disagree with a sociology professor about gay marriage. _____
2. Call your conservative Christian roommate "closed minded." _____
3. Decline a date with a person you find uninteresting. _____
4. Participate in an antiterrorism demonstration where participants burn a Quran. _____
5. Drive while intoxicated. _____
6. Volunteer to canvass neighborhoods for a political campaign. _____
7. Shout profanities at an opposing team during a football game. _____
8. Plagiarize a paper from another student who completed the same class. _____
9. Spread a rumor about the sexual orientation of a classmate on Facebook. _____
10. Share alcohol with your underage friends. _____

The Civility Index

Think about the definition of *civility* as presented in this chapter. Now apply it to yourself and your interactions with others at school, at work, and in your community. After reading each statement below, circle the number that best reflects how you view your civility. There are no wrong answers. This is simply a way to reflect on the meaning of civility and how you employ it in your daily life. Once you have finished, total your responses and find where you fall on the Civility Index.

NEVER	SOMETIMES	ALWAYS

1. I stop during busy traffic to allow other drivers to enter my lane.

1	2	3	4	5

2. When addressing a stranger, I use "sir" or "ma'am."

1	2	3	4	5

3. I try harder to hear what someone else is trying to say than to get across my point.

1	2	3	4	5

4. I engage in small volunteer acts, such as making a meal for a friend, holding the door for others, or giving up my seat for a pregnant woman.

1	2	3	4	5

5. I attend neighborhood association or campus community meetings.

1	2	3	4	5

6. I am a member of a parent-teacher or student association.

1	2	3	4	5

7. I do not text or check e-mail on my phone while someone is speaking to me.

1   2   3   4   5

8. I do not read tabloid magazines.

1   2   3   4   5

9. I apologize when I have hurt someone.

1   2   3   4   5

10. I admit when I am wrong.

1   2   3   4   5

11. I think that a person's viewpoints are not a direct reflection of character.

1   2   3   4   5

12. I have written to a government official or a newspaper regarding a public issue.

1   2   3   4   5

13. I respect and support police officers.

1   2   3   4   5

14. I volunteer for political campaigns.

1   2   3   4   5

15. I say "hello" to strangers.

1   2   3   4   5

16. When I see a homeless person asking for money or selling something, I contribute.

1   2   3   4   5

17. If I see a student or friend being harassed by another, I intervene.

1   2   3   4   5

18. I feel it is more important to lead by consensus than by decree.

1   2   3   4   5

19. I feel comfortable around people who are completely different from me.

1   2   3   4   5

20. I do not freely express my opinions when I know it will offend others.

1   2   3   4   5

21. I do not wear T-shirts with controversial messages.

1   2   3   4   5

22. I organize celebrations for the achievements or milestones in my friends' lives.

1   2   3   4   5

23. I educate myself on the records and stances of political candidates before I vote as opposed to voting based purely on party affiliations.

1   2   3   4   5

24. I believe that there is a solution to every problem if thought and action are invested.

1   2   3   4   5

25. I am aware of the issues faced by lower-income and poverty-stricken members of my community.

1   2   3   4   5

Enter Total Score

Civility Index – Interpreting Your Score

25 – 49: This range indicates a lower level of civil behavior. There is an ebb and flow to the frenetic pace of modern life. You may be in a period of high stress with many obligations and little time for volunteering or focusing on the needs of others. Perhaps you engage in uncivil behaviors that you have come to view as acceptable because so many others do. Whatever the case may be, a score below 50 may indicate that you should be more cognizant of the way you treat others or take small steps toward more community engagement.

50 – 75: Congratulations! Civility is a part of your daily life. One would imagine that most people fall in this range. You may volunteer a couple of times each year or routinely engage in small acts of civility throughout your day. For the most part, your interactions with others are polite and thoughtful. In other words, you're not Mother Teresa, but you're doing a pretty good job. You are mindful of the people around you and treat them with respect. Although you may not always have the opportunity, time, or resources to serve or give back to the community, civility is important to you.

76 – 125: Wow! You are either running for public office or about to reach sainthood. You place an extremely high value on civility and make it a high priority in your life. This kind of dedication and effort, in combination with action, is to be lauded and serves as an example for others. Be careful of burnout. When you are constantly giving of yourself, people may take your goodwill for granted. When civility is not reciprocated, maintaining this high level of civility may become more difficult. Stay strong.

DISCLAIMER: This test and index are not a scientifically precise measure of civility but a gauge by which to compare behavior and thoughts on civility. Measuring civility is difficult if not nearly impossible and in some cases may be very subjective.

The Democrats are the party of government activism,
the party that says government can make you richer,
smarter, taller, and get the chickweed out of your lawn.
Republicans are the party that says the government does
not work, and then get elected and prove it.
—P. J. O'Rourke

CHAPTER 2

Uncivil Political Discourse

Today people talk about political issues without regard to offending others. It is hard to think about incivility in America without first discussing the political rancor and vitriol that are so pervasive. We have reached a point where the ideological divide is so great between political factions, it seems almost impossible for our political leaders to make important decisions about our future.

Too many politicians see consensus as compromise. Their goal is to dominate the opposition. Instead of seriously considering opposing ideas, protagonists make personal attacks on their opponents—often without merit. This good-versus-evil mentality in politics is not helpful and leads to further incivility. Incivility is often fueled by constituents and public interest groups that provide support to politicians who take hard-line stances. The end result is political gridlock and deeply divided communities. Lost in all the commotion is the fact that despite our differences we are all united as Americans.

Many American citizens are fed up with the current level of partisan polarization in politics. According to the Pew Research Center for People in the Press, Americans are more polarized today than at any point in the past twenty-five years.[1]

Important societal issues such as immigration, climate change, health care reform, government spending, job creation, gay marriage, and gun control have resulted in a deep partisan divide. Impassioned debate over these issues tends to digress into below-the-belt attacks against opposition or take-it-or-leave-it propositions that fail before they ever get off the ground.

Politicians accuse their opponents of being "liars," "traitors," and even "Nazis." Ideas of opposition parties are labeled "un-American" or "stupid." This type of inflammatory commentary is pervasive in cable news programming, talk radio, social media, and blogs. Noticeably lacking in our political discourse is any semblance of respect for diverse ideas or meaningful consensus. Instead, competing factions use the political process to vilify each other and try to score political points.

Could the uncivil conduct of our political leaders contribute to incivility that is rampant throughout society? Are citizens mirroring the outlandish behavior of many of our elected leaders? With so many Americans outraged by the dysfunctional political environment, many believe we can and *must* do better.

According to the latest Civility in America poll conducted by Politico, a whopping 81 percent of those surveyed believed incivility in our government is "harming America's future."[2] Perhaps this response should come as no surprise. Politicians know how to leverage the media by making inflammatory comments and engaging in outlandish conduct. Politicians know that over-the-top political theater attracts media attention. This conduct is then rebroadcast through cable news, talk radio, blogs, and social media and is discussed by citizens over coffee and around the water cooler. Like a bad reality television program, the entertainment value associated with watching unruly politicians is irresistible.

Competing political factions do not just disagree on policy—they genuinely dislike each other. This animosity becomes a roadblock to consensus and meaningful compromise. Worse yet, many citizens choose to mirror the uncivil rhetoric, attitudes, and behavior of their political leaders. Hostility is not confined to politicians and the political process; it encompasses millions of Americans with diverse values and beliefs. The politicians are the standard bearers for citizens who elect representatives to fight for their ideals.

There have been calls for greater civility in political discourse from political leaders, such as President Barack Obama and others. Several nonprofits have emerged to promote and encourage civility in politics. For example, the National Institute for Civil Discourse focuses on encouraging "thoughtful national dialogue" between Congress and the executive branch of government.[3]

This chapter analyzes civility and incivility historically in American politics. Assessing the current acrimonious political environment should not be done in a vacuum. Democracy tends to be inherently messy. Incivility has been a part of politics from the very beginning of our Union. This chapter also assesses the political values and beliefs held by students in the Millennial generation.

TURMOIL OVER GUN DEBATE: SONAM

Now in her sophomore year, Sonam began to recognize her affinity for political advocacy. During her freshman year she had participated in a Take Back the Night protest bringing awareness to the issue of sexual violence against women. She also served as a leader of the International Student Club (ISC). As a foreign-born national of Indian descent, Sonam found that the ISC provided an outlet to connect with similar international students and bring greater awareness on campus to issues ranging from diversity to immigration.

Sonam's active involvement in the campus community was empowering. She *really* believed that she could make a difference to improve the campus culture. So when Sonam discovered the Political Engagement Club, she knew she had to join. The club was a relatively new nonpartisan student organization that focused on increasing political awareness and engagement on campus. Unlike the campus Democrat and Republican organizations, which in Sonam's mind were blindly aligned with a political platform, the Political Engagement Club might offer genuine opportunities for discussion about important political issues.

Sonam's first meeting with the club was even better than she expected. About ten other students were in attendance, and they all seemed to share a disdain for the current climate of political polarization. Everyone seemed very personable, and several of the students took the time to introduce themselves, including the club's cofounder and leader, Kevin Nichols.

When Kevin first noticed Sonam, he immediately introduced himself. "Hi. My name is Kevin. Thanks for coming out tonight."

Sonam had just taken a bite of the free pizza the club provided for the meeting and was unable to respond immediately.

Kevin said, "Sorry. Perfect timing I guess. I can't help it. I'm also a server at Applebee's. We have a knack for asking questions when our guests have food in their mouths!"

Kevin was tall and thin with dark brown hair that hung in his face like a mop. He wore circle wire-rimmed glasses reminiscent of Harry Potter's. Despite his somewhat geeky physique, Kevin carried himself with confidence. He wore khaki pants with a white shirt and a necktie that had the constitution written on it. It was clear that he was the leader of this group of political misfits.

Sonam chuckled as she quickly swallowed her bite of pizza. "My name is Sonam. Sonam Mahra, but please just call me Sonam."

"Hey, Sonam!" Kevin replied

"How long have you guys been meeting?" Sonam asked.

"We started a few months ago. Since then we have been working to get our message out around campus. We have built a mean and lean core group that is committed to nonpartisan engagement. We've gotten a lot of positive student feedback! In fact tonight we have a major announcement regarding our first event. It should definitely get us on the map."

Sonam replied, "Sweet! I can't wait."

Kevin smiled and said, "If you have any questions about our club, please let me know. I really appreciate you taking to the time to attend."

Sonam felt an instant connection with this group. She wondered what the "major announcement" might be as the meeting began. Whatever it was, she definitely wanted to get in on the action.

After mingling informally over pizza and soft drinks, everyone took their seats and Kevin began the meeting. Following a brief welcome and introduction, he explained to the group, "I've got big news! Our request to hold a panel discussion on gun control has been approved by Student Affairs!"

The atmosphere became electric in the room as students clapped their hands and gave each other high fives. The club had apparently been working to get this event off the ground for the last three weeks.

Kevin continued, "The administration likes our idea and is allowing us to use a large lecture auditorium in the political science building that seats 250."

Sonam loved the idea. Gun control was one of those complex and very controversial issues that did not lend itself to a simple solution. Sonam thought, *Perhaps an intelligent campus discussion on the issue would be helpful in exploring solutions for this issue.*

Kevin explained that several prominent faculty members had volunteered to participate on the panel. Although the Political Engagement Club would be hosting the event, it would be working hand in hand with the campus Democrat and Republican clubs, as well as another student club called Students for the Rights to Bear Arms (SRBA). The goal of the panel discussion was to present the issue in a nonpartisan manner, offering perspective both for and against gun control measures. By involving faculty and other student clubs, the group would be able to increase its reach exponentially and was likely to garner publicity from the campus paper and local press.

The issue of gun control had received a lot of media attention over the last several weeks as a deranged gunman had opened fire at a shopping mall in Oregon, killing five people and injuring dozens of others, including children. The gunman ultimately killed himself before he was captured by authorities. The shooting made national news and ignited a national debate on stricter gun control legislation.

Sonam was in. She volunteered to help with marketing the event on campus, which included creating flyers and using a social media blitz. She also helped with developing questions for the panelists. There was a buzz on campus about the event. Word got out that some of the professors were offering extra credit to students who attended the event. More than likely the auditorium would be filled.

Things were moving along smoothly until the night of the event. It appeared that students did not want to listen to a reasoned policy discussion on gun control but preferred to make a political statement. Leading the charge was the SRBA, which had organized a large rally of nearly fifty raucous students outside the political science building holding signs with inflammatory rhetoric. One sign read, "Ban Ignorance, not Guns," and another read, "All in favor of gun control raise your right hand," below a picture of Adolf Hitler with his right arm fully extended in a salute and a red swastika on his left arm.

Not to be outdone, the campus Democrat club had rallied an equally rowdy group of protesters toting their own signs, chanting slogans, and making a scene. One sign had a picture of an AR-15 semiautomatic rifle with a caption that read, "Is this REALLY what the Founding Fathers had in mind?" Another sign simply read, "Don't tase me bro!"

Before long, the local media showed up at the event. It seemed that with journalists on hand and cameras rolling, the protesters felt the need to amp up their outlandish conduct. Protesters flung insults at each other. Vitriolic words, such as "fascist," "racist," "Nazi," "murderer," and "stupid," could be made out above the mass of voices, all screaming at once, vying to get attention. The hostilities escalated when someone from the pro-gun control side "accidentally" threw a half-filled plastic water bottle into the SRBA's rally. Instantly, several scuffles and fights broke out. More bottles, rocks, and other projectiles were hurled between the two sides. The chanting and screaming intensified to pushing and shoving. Campus security immediately moved in to break up the fights and attempted to disperse the students peacefully.

Standing at the second-floor window of the political science building, the members of the Political Engagement Club watched the events unfold in absolute disbelief. The blue lights from the campus police cruisers illuminated the front of the building as campus security forces worked to restore order. The protesting students quickly realized the show was over and dispersed. In the aftermath, trash and trampled signs lay cluttered on the ground. Journalists and camera crews were scurrying around, interviewing students and questioning the campus police. The administration canceled the event.

Several students were arrested, but they had a look of pride on their faces. They seemed satisfied with themselves for exercising their rights to free speech and fighting for their convictions. Dismayed, Sonam thought, *What was gained? How did it go so wrong?*

HISTORICAL PERSPECTIVE

The ideological battle that Sonam witnessed over the issue of gun control is consistent with our political heritage. While the current status of political discourse is unquestionably troubling, there has never been a "golden age" of purely constructive discourse in American politics.[4] Rancor has been endemic in the democratic system of governance.[5] From the very inception of our country, there were concerns about incivility in government. In 1776 John Adams expressed his fears that the members of the Continental Congress would obtain "influence by noise, not sense. By meanness, not greatness. By ignorance, not learning. By contracted hearts, not large souls."[6]

John Adams's sentiments were prophetic. Even in his own presidential reelection campaign in 1800, civility was noticeably lacking. With the exception of mass media coverage, the tone of the presidential election of 1800 between the incumbent John Adams and Thomas Jefferson was not much different from the presidential elections of modern times. Adams accused Jefferson of being "a howling atheist," whose sympathy for the French Revolution would bring chaos to the country.[7] Jefferson denounced Adams's love of federal power, specifically the imposition of new taxes and deficit spending.[8] The partisan press called Adams "a hideous hermaphroditical character" and Jefferson "a mean-spirited, low-life fellow, the son of a half-breed squaw."[9]

The presidential election of 1828 between the incumbent John Quincy Adams and Andrew Jackson was also marked by dirty political tactics. The campaign was filled with intense personal character attacks by both the candidates and their supporters. Opponents called John Quincy Adams a "pimp" based on an unsubstantiated rumor that Adams had procured an American girl for sexual services for the Russian czar during his tenure as a Russian ambassador. Adams supporters referred to Andrew Jackson as "Andrew Jackass," accused Jackson of adultery, and alleged that he executed six militia members accused of desertion during the War of 1812.[10]

The years leading up to the Civil War were particularly tumultuous for American politics. The United States was torn apart over the issue of slavery. The abolitionist movement was becoming increasingly vocal, and enormous controversy was focused on whether new states admitted to the Union would allow slavery. The political hostility between politicians who supported or opposed slavery during the 1850s makes the current political wrangling look like child's play. Members of the House of Representatives and the Senate were known to wrestle and engage in fist fights during legislative sessions over issues involving slavery.[11]

For example, in 1856, abolitionist Senator Charles Sumner of Massachusetts was nearly beaten to death with a heavy cane on the Senate floor by Preston Brooks, a member of the House of Representatives from South Carolina. Brooks was incensed by a powerful speech delivered by Sumner denouncing the Kansas-Nebraska Act that allowed new states to decide whether to make slavery legal. Sumner's speech criticized Andrew Pickens Butler, a South Carolina senator who had coauthored the Kansas-Nebraska Act. Prior to beating Sumner, Brooks declared, "You have libeled my State and slandered my relation who is aged and absent and I feel it to be my duty to punish you for it!"[12]

In the 1930s, opponents of President Franklin Roosevelt regularly accused him of being "un-American" or a "Communist" in response to his New Deal legislation.

In the 1950s, states grappled with the implementation of *Brown v. Board of Education,* which held that racial segregation in public schools was unconstitutional. In 1963, Alabama Governor George Wallace famously vowed "segregation now, segregation tomorrow, and segregation forever."[13] Wallace's sentiments were representative of many Americans during the civil rights movement of the 1960s.[14]

During the civil rights era, African Americans challenged the ingrained culture of racial discrimination and segregation, creating social upheaval. Students participated in demonstrations and boycotts. In reaction, churches were bombed and key civil right leaders such as Malcolm X and Martin Luther King Jr. were assassinated.[15]

The end of the 1960s saw a growing antiwar movement as public support for the war in Viet Nam waned.[16] College students played a major role in these war protests. The antiwar movement actually began on college campuses. Antiwar sentiment began to build as more Americans were drafted to serve in the armed forces and as American casualties rose. The average age of a soldier serving in Viet Nam was only nineteen. Protesters became more vocal in criticizing the government's war policies. One protest chant that was particularly damaging to President Lyndon B. Johnson was, "Hey! Hey! LBJ! How many kids did you kill today?"

A turning point in the antiwar movement occurred in 1970 during a protracted student protest at Kent State University.[17] Students protested President Nixon's decision to send troops into Cambodia. The four-day protest ended tragically when National Guard troops opened fire on the protesting students, leaving four dead and many more injured. In the ensuing outcry, many colleges and universities closed their doors before the end of the term in order to avoid protests and possible violence.

DEVELOPING A NEW MODEL FOR POLITICAL DISCOURSE

Given our acrimonious political history, many wonder whether Americans are even capable of a more civil political discourse. Is political influence obtained by "meanness, not greatness" as John Adams feared? Clearly, this was Sonam's experience.

While it is highly unlikely that there will ever be a time when competing political factions will be able to hold hands and sing "Kum Ba Yah" after hammering out a piece of legislation, we can do better. Perhaps the fact that today's political discord *rarely* results in duels, fist fights, or canings is evidence that we have learned something from our wild and unruly past.

Taming our tongues presents difficult challenges given the First Amendment protections afforded to free speech and expression. *Legally,* we may be able to verbally lambaste people with opposing political views, but the bigger issue is whether anything constructive is achieved by doing so. Clearly, political tough talking and hostile antics toward opposition can energize certain constituents who are ideologically aligned. For example, U.S. Representative Joseph Wilson's famous "You lie!" outburst during President Barack Obama's 2009 State of the Union address resulted in donations totaling more than $1 million from individuals opposed to health care reform.[18] However, did the outburst lead to any substantive reevaluation of the proposed legislation? Did it challenge those who supported the legislation to reconsider their positions? Did any counter proposals emanate from the comment? When policy development is based on who can make the most noise, meaningful collaboration is lost.

Improving political discourse requires developing a new model of political engagement, according to Susan Herbst.[19] She argues in *Rude Democracy: Civility and Incivility in American Politics* that one approach to improving political discourse is to create a "culture of listening." So much of political debate is based on being heard. This means talking, yelling, even screaming over others. Everyone wants to talk at once. However, very little time is spent listening to others and processing information intelligently.

Doing this requires teaching political leaders and the population how to argue with vigor but also with mutual respect.

Herbst suggests that political discourse needs "rules of evidence."[20] In the information age, anyone can say anything and have it broadcast with little or no verification. Without common rules of evidence, the public can be easily duped by half-truths and misinformation. Incorrect information can take on a life of its own. Ascertaining the veracity of information can be difficult when information is filtered through partisan media outlets. Most people experience information overload. Going directly to the legislative source often requires milling through hundreds of pages of legalese, which may generate even more confusion. Policy debates and public opinion are often based on short video clips, sound bites, and cherry-picked information repeated by politicians and political pundits.

A new model of political discourse acknowledges that disagreement is inherent to the democratic process. Civility does not require emotionless neutrality. Competing ideas can be fully and passionately presented, argued, challenged, and debated with mutual respect. Not all impassioned disagreement constitutes incivility. Constructive disagreement requires fair and balanced assessment of information. Debaters offer robust and fair critiques, avoid scare tactics and intentional obfuscation of information, and analyze the substance of policy and ideas openly. Stakeholders speak and also listen to others. Speakers ratchet down inflammatory rhetoric and do not engage in vitriolic personal attacks.

When our political leaders learn to lead with civility and mutual respect, perhaps opposing sides will be able to work together for the common good. Modeling this behavior may also prompt constituents to do the same. Over time politicians and the general public will come to understand the benefits of more civil engagement. While it is very likely that conservatives, liberals, and independents will have divergent views on policy, efforts to find common ground should be paramount. When compromise is reached, opposing sides should respect the final outcome as a legitimate outcome of a democratic process.

LIVING IN A BUBBLE

What is the effect of political incivility on communities? Bryan Gervais argues that political incivility breeds distrust and substantially lowers the perspective of people who hold opposing views. According to Gervais, people exposed to uncivil media tend to "mirror that incivility." When uncivil political discourse receives extensive media coverage, it essentially "legitimizes the use of uncivil language and behavior."[21]

It seems only natural that communities form around common beliefs and values. However, sometimes these communities can become so insular and self-absorbed that they never interact with others who do not share the same beliefs and values. They become isolated from others in the larger community. These isolated subcommunities operate within a bubble. People inside the bubble create their own reality. They are inclined to surround themselves only with people who share their perspectives; they constantly feed themselves with information that supports their views; and they see others who are outside their bubble as inferior or misguided.

Many bubbles exist within a community—political parties, religious sects, minority and ethnic groups, and groups that are based on socioeconomic status. To a certain extent, each bubble has its own political agenda. The bubble provides a filter through which others outside are viewed. Sometimes engagement between members of conflicting bubbles is based on unfair preconceived notions created within the bubble. This extremely narrow application of community based on self-segregation does not promote mutual respect or true community engagement.

In a democratic society, we are free to express our beliefs and associate with like-minded persons. Clearly, we are entitled to disagree with others' views. In the context of civil political engagement, the issue is, How do people disagree with others or challenge their beliefs in a way that is productive and does not involve uncivil tactics?

The first step is to pierce the bubbles and acknowledge that others are entitled to their own perspectives. We must expand our definition of community engagement to include others who may not share our values, beliefs, and political affiliations. When we confront differences, it may also be helpful to recognize the merit of others' positions and attempt to understand why a person holds a particular position. When we extend respect and courtesy to people with different beliefs and values, the tone of the discourse is likely to change. *The key is respect.* Perhaps when we learn to respect the diverse political views of the people in our community, meaningful engagement and expanded learning can occur. We may learn that we are similar in more ways than we are different.

MILLENNIALS

Generations, like people, have personalities. The Millennial generation—some of whom are in college—now making its passage into adulthood has begun to forge its own unique identity. Examining the makeup, values, and tendencies of the Millennial generation is important to understanding students on campuses today and the future of political discourse. This up-and-coming generation will be a significant group to understand when projecting the trajectory of policy and political engagement.

According to the Pew Research Center, Millennials tend to be confident, self-expressive, liberal, upbeat, and open to change.[22] They are more ethnically and racially diverse than other adults. They are less religious, are less likely to have served in the military, and are on track to become the most educated generation in American history. The education trend is driven largely by the demands of a modern knowledge-based economy but has accelerated in recent years by the lack of jobs.

Unemployment rates are the highest among Millennials. In fact, more than 10 percent of older Millennials have "boomeranged" back to a parent's home because of the recession. Despite their struggle to find employment, about 90 percent of Millennials either say that they currently have enough money or that they will eventually meet their long-term financial goals. Millennials tend to be more optimistic than their elders about their own economic future as well as about the overall state of the nation.[23]

Millennials remain the most likely of any generation to self-identify as liberals; they are less supportive of an assertive national security policy and more supportive of a progressive domestic social agenda.[24]

Millennials embrace multiple modes of self-expression—especially through technology. For example, 24 percent of Millennials say they are distinctive from other generations because of their use of technology. The overwhelming majority have created a profile on social networking sites. About 20 percent have posted a video of themselves online.[25]

Only about 60 percent of Millennials were raised by both parents—a smaller share than was the case with older generations. However, they tend to get along well with their parents. Looking back at their teenage years, Millennials report having had fewer spats with mom or dad than older adults say they had with their own parents when they were growing up.[26]

Politically, Millennials were among Barack Obama's strongest supporters in 2008. Approximately 66 percent of Millennials backed Obama for president, while just 50 percent of older adults voted for the Democratic nominee. This was the largest disparity between younger and older voters recorded in four decades of modern Election Day exit polling. Moreover, after decades of low voter participation by the young, the turnout gap in 2008 between voters under and over the age of thirty was the smallest it had been since eighteen-to twenty-year-olds were given the right to vote in 1972.[27]

During the 2012 presidential election, Millennial participation bumped up 1 percent over the 2008 presidential election.[28] In 2012, Millennials represented approximately 21 percent of the voting eligible population.[29] Of this 21 percent, about 19 percent voted in the 2012 presidential election.[30] The data shows that Millennials continue to be politically engaged.

According to a study conducted by the Center for Information & Research on Civic Learning & Engagement (CIRCLE), Millennial college students are more politically engaged than Generation X, which preceded them. Generation X considered politics irrelevant and generally saw little purpose in actively participating in the political system.[31] Millennials tend to take a less cynical view. Millennials are likely to have a great deal of experience with volunteerism and feel obligated to work together with others on social issues.

While Generation X tended to ignore partisan political rancor, Millennials dislike partisan spin and polarized debates and instead seek "authentic" opportunities to discuss political issues.[32] This might explain Sonam's desire to join the nonpartisan Political Engagement Club in the opening vignette. Millennials express a desire to understand political issues, yet at the same time are very skeptical of news and information from sources with a partisan bent.[33] The issue is not a lack of information but a dearth of news and opinion they trust.

The unique personality of the Millennial generation may provide hope for more civil discourse in the future. Millennials tend to express more comfort with diversity and change. The ability to respect diverse people and ideas is critical to facilitating civil political discourse. The ability to change may mean that younger voters will not be so entrenched that they are unwilling to work toward consensus. Record high voter turnout over the last two presidential elections and the general optimism that Millennials express about the current state of the nation demonstrate an increased level of civic responsibility and genuine interest in the political process. Millennials could be instrumental in changing the uncivil political tone that is so often deafening.

STUDENT POLITICAL ENGAGEMENT

College students and college campuses are often ground zero for political activism. There has been a movement at many institutions to facilitate student political involvement. From student political clubs to campus rallies, symposiums, and events featuring prominent political leaders, there are usually many opportunities for students to participate in the political process.

Students may spearhead voter registration drives or organize voting trips where students sign up to travel together to the polls and vote as a group. Students may also volunteer to canvass for a politician or a political party. This might include making phone calls, passing out flyers, talking to other students and the community about a political issue, or spreading the word about a politician they support via social media.

Higher education institutions can play a critical role in political and civil engagement of students through curricular programs and extracurricular activities. Relevant course content based on current events, public policy, and civic influences tends to trigger student interest in political involvement. Integrating community service opportunities is also linked with students' increased civic and political engagement.[34] Some students choose to volunteer long-term in organizations such as City Year or the Peace Corps. Others choose to use spring and summer breaks to participate in volunteerism, ranging from animal rescues in the Amazon rain forest to teaching orphan children in developing countries.

The bottom line is that politically engaged youth are likely to continue to be politically engaged as adults. Early exposure to political engagement and community service may lead to an increase in meaningful adult political participation. These types of early experiences provide students with opportunities to meet diverse people and see firsthand other communities and challenges that people encounter daily.

Like the Millennials, other Americans long for more authentic political discourse. Perhaps the tides are beginning to change.

TOOLS AND EXERCISES

What Went Wrong?

Review the vignette, "Turmoil Over Gun Debate," at the beginning of chapter 2 featuring Sonam and the Political Engagement Club. Think about the various actors involved in creating the campus event, their expectations, and the outcome. After reviewing the material discussed in chapter 2, think about what went wrong and answer the following questions:

1. What do you think the Political Engagement Club could have done differently, if anything, to prepare for the outcome of the event?

2. Did the Political Engagement Club err by including outside groups in the debate? Explain.

3. What could the university have done differently on the front end of the debate?

4. Do you think campus security should have been more involved? How might that have changed the tone of the event?

5. Do you think the protesters' exercise of their freedom of speech had meaning or impact? Do you think responsibility comes with the freedom of speech?

6. Do you think that canceling the event was the best way for the university to handle the conflict?

7. How could the Political Engagement Club, the university, and the other clubs involved have turned this situation into something positive or created a constructive dialogue about it?

Historical Interpretation

Rank the following five historical events from "least" to "most" in terms of civility. There is no correct order, only your interpretation of history as it relates to examples of civility. Explain your rankings.

_____ *The Boston Tea Party:* In 1773, the Sons of Liberty, a group of American colonists, boarded ships in Boston Harbor belonging to the East India Company and destroyed its shipment of tea by throwing it into the ocean. This was in response to the Tea Act (1773) passed by the British Parliament, taxing all tea imported into the American colonies.[35]

_____ *The Bombing of Hiroshima:* In an effort to end World War II, Harry Truman announced on August 6, 1945, to the American public that an atomic bomb had been dropped on the Japanese city of Hiroshima. The bomb killed an estimated 60,000 to 80,000 people instantly, with the ultimate death toll at 135,000.[36]

_____ *1989 Flag burning:* In protest of the Flag Protection Act of 1989, which made desecration of the American flag illegal, four people burned flags on the steps of the U.S. Capitol. This led to the U.S. Supreme Court case, *United States v. Eichman* (1990), in which the Flag Protection Act was ruled a violation of First Amendment rights.[37]

_____ *The Los Angeles riots:* The highly publicized 1992 trial of four Los Angeles police officers found not guilty of police brutality in the beating of Rodney King resulted in a city-wide race riot lasting six days, in which stores were bombed and looted and more than two thousand were injured and fifty-three were killed.[38]

_____ *Death of Princess Diana:* In 1997, after being pursued at high speeds by seven photographers on motorcycles, the car carrying Diana crashed in a Paris tunnel, killing her companion and bodyguard instantly. Diana died two hours later in a Paris hospital. While it was found that the driver of the car had been under the influence of drugs and alcohol, the behavior of the press was criticized and came under intense scrutiny.[39]

It used to be that when children didn't get their way, they would throw a temper tantrum. Now we are seeing adults behaving the same way. That seems to be a troubling trend: If we don't get our way, we resort to crazy behavior.

—**Mark DeMoss,**
Founder of the Civility Project

CHAPTER 3

Popular Culture's Effect on Civility

"You are what you eat." This saying could also apply to a person's media consumption. From a young age, we are inundated with various forms of media that glorify uncivil and boorish behavior. It is hard to imagine a hit television program or blockbuster movie that does not involve profanity, violence, and sexual innuendo. Top-selling recording artists fill the radio airwaves and ear buds with raunchy lyrics focusing on self-indulgence, lewdness, and materialism. Some of the most popular video games provide players with the vivid first-person sensation of wreaking havoc in realistic virtual worlds with ultraviolent and "adult" content.

News outlets provide constant breaking news of crime in our communities and atrocities around the globe. Outrageous conduct and scandals involving celebrities, athletes, and politicians make headlines and clutter social media. While there are many more civil aspects of our society that are newsworthy, they simply do not garner ratings.

Shocking and controversial media gets the most intrigue, attention, and viewers.

The media in America enjoys robust First Amendment protections and rightfully so. While the media tends to focus on the more uncivil aspects of our society, these subjects usually have legitimate artistic, entertainment, and political value and are therefore protected under the First Amendment. Freedom to express controversial information, ideas, and beliefs is essential in a free and open society.

The scope and reach of the media today are unprecedented. People have twenty-four-hour media access on multiple platforms. According to a national survey conducted by the Kaiser Family Foundation, teens spend more than seven hours a day consuming media.[1] Media consumption includes watching television, listening to music, surfing the Internet, social networking, and playing video games. According to the Bureau of Labor Statistics, watching television is the leisure activity that occupies the most time among adults.[2] According to Nielsen, young adults watch twenty-five hours of television each week.[3] The amount of time in front of the television steadily increases with age. For example, adults over sixty-five watch an average of forty-eight hours of television each week.[4]

How does our excessive appetite for media affect our behavior and attitudes toward others—particularly when the content we consume is increasingly uncivil? Media experts estimate that 90 percent of movies, 68 percent of video games, and 60 percent of television programs show some depictions of violence.[5] Media content popular with teens and young adults often contains heavy doses of sexual content, such as touching, kissing, and engaging in intercourse.[6] Divisive political rhetoric on television and radio is especially shrill as candidates and pundits vilify their opposition, often with below-the-belt tactics.[7] Shocking stories of celebrity narcissism and bad behavior make news headlines and are the subjects of international interest.

Evidence suggests that the media we consume is influencing community values regarding such things as relationships, gender roles, body image, politics, and even clothing. Does the nonstop incivility we see in the media truly represent our culture? Is our culture negatively influenced by the uncivil media we consume, or is the media merely reflecting the pervasive incivility that exists independent of media influences? Can we truly separate our identity and conduct from the powerful effects of media that vies for our attention? This chapter explores how popular culture, through various forms of media, can play a significant role in doing civility.

YOU'RE ONLY YOUNG ONCE: LINDSEY

The 9 percent tuition increase was like a punch in the stomach to the thousands of students who were already taking out loans to finance their education. Lindsey's roommate, Megan, was particularly hard hit. Megan's dad had recently lost his job, and her parents were no longer able to pay her tuition and school expenses. Inspired by her dad's story of working his way through college, Megan was determined to stay in school and pay her own way *without* taking out additional student loans.

Megan quickly landed a customer service job working the front desk at a hotel on campus, but it did not take long for Megan to realize that her part-time salary did not come close to covering her expenses. Even more challenging was keeping up with her schoolwork. Soon she discovered a new level of exhaustion. Managing her full-time college schedule and almost full-time job was beyond demanding. Her social life also took a major hit. Megan knew that if she was going to finish her undergraduate degree and get into medical school, she would need to be resourceful and think outside the box. She was desperate.

Lindsey was genuinely concerned for her roommate. The two friends had enjoyed hanging out, shopping, and partying together on weekends. Unfortunately, Megan's new reality began to strain her relationship with Lindsey. Megan rarely had free time to do anything, and when she did she was cranky, agitated, and not much fun to be around.

After weeks of being AWOL from the campus social scene, Megan abruptly reemerged with a vengeance. Her evenings and weekends suddenly became free, and her attitude seemed to change. Instead of constantly stressing about money, Megan seemed to be carefree. In fact, all indications were that money was no longer an issue. She completely abandoned her newfound thriftiness for extravagant shopping sprees, eating out with friends, and even splurging on jewelry.

Lindsey was pretty sure Megan had quit her part-time job. She assumed that Megan's dad found a new, better job, or perhaps a relative was helping her out financially. She did not want to pry into Megan's personal business, but she became suspicious of the radical turn of events. Equally suspicious was the fact that Megan got dressed up to go out every Wednesday and Thursday after class—really dressed up. She would not tell anyone where she was going. On these evenings she would often be out late. Lindsey had no idea what Megan was doing. She suspected there might be a new guy in the picture, although she wondered why Megan was being so secretive. Dating cute guys on campus was always a topic of conversation between roommates.

One Thursday night, Lindsey was up working at her desk on a term paper when Megan came in around 11:30 p.m. Her outfit, hair, and makeup looked as if she had been out with someone.

Peering over the screen of her laptop, Lindsey asked, "So, are you and Mason back together again?"

Megan responded, "No! We're over. Why do you ask?"

"I don't know," replied Lindsey. "I just thought you might have been out with someone."

"Maybe I was," said Megan with a slight smirk on her face.

"Okay, I see how you are," Lindsey said with a bit of sarcasm as she closed her laptop computer. "If you don't want to tell your roomie what's going on, that's cool. I just don't want to come home and find some strange guy roaming around our suite."

Megan replied, "Don't worry, Linz, you know I'd give you at least a ten-minute warning."

As Megan walked over to the minifridge to grab a Diet Dr. Pepper, Lindsey immediately noticed Megan's outfit and said, "No way! Are those Dylan George jeans?"

Megan replied, "Yeah, I just got them today! Aren't they cute?"

"Cute?" replied Lindsey, partly in shock, "Yeah, they're cute, but did you rob a bank or something! And is that a Louis Vuitton handbag? I thought you were trying to save your money?"

Megan suddenly became very quiet.

"Look, Megan," Lindsey said firmly, "you've been acting strange the last couple weeks. What's going on?"

Megan knew that at some point Lindsey was likely to ask about her unusual change of circumstances. She immediately wished that she had been more discreet. Megan had really wanted to talk to Lindsey, but she was embarrassed. After a long, awkward moment of silence, Megan dropped her Louis Vuitton bag on her desk and replied quietly, "Okay, so maybe I met someone online . . . someone who's a little older than me."

"Don't tell me you're hooking up with one of your managers at the hotel."

"No," replied Megan as she sank into her Big Joe Bean Bag chair perpendicular to Lindsey's desk. "I'm not hooking up with anyone. His name is Robert," she said. "He's a heart surgeon at the community hospital."

"Seriously, you're dating a doctor!" Lindsey exclaimed.

"Well, we're not really dating," Megan replied, "we're just friends. He's new to the area and is looking for companionship—someone to hang out with. He's really nice and *very* supportive."

"Supportive?" Lindsey asked. "So is your new companion buying you all these new expensive clothes and accessories?"

"Look, Linz, it's not what you think. I mean, he's married. He's just looking for someone to, you know, spend time with and pamper . . . I don't know, kind of like a daughter."

"Wait a minute. He's married!" Lindsey could not believe what she was hearing. "He needs to be hanging out with his wife! How old is this guy anyway?"

"I think he's in his forties, but he really just wants to help. I mean, he already paid my tuition for the rest of the semester, and he's willing to give me five thousand dollars if I go with him to a seminar next weekend in Boston. He thought it would be really helpful for me to sit in during the presentations."

"Please tell me you're not going," Lindsey stated. "This is just way too creepy."

"Stop judging me," Megan said defensively. "I thought you would understand. Look, I need money. I'll never be able to afford tuition working on campus. If my parents can't pay for my education, I'm on my own. Who else is going to help? You know I want to get into medical school. Robert is like a mentor, and he is offering to support me financially. All I need to do is spend a little time with him during the week. He takes really good care of me. I know the whole arrangement looks a little weird from the outside, and maybe he does not see me as a daughter, but our relationship is not bad—it's mutually beneficial. I'm not the only one who's doing this. There are legit Web sites out there that help people like me find supportive relationships. I'm only going to be young once. I may as well take advantage of it while I can."

Megan stormed off to her room and closed the door behind her. Lindsey was in shock. She knew that she had offended her friend even though she was not trying to judge; however, this whole situation gave her an icky feeling. Lindsey admired the fact that Megan was trying to pay her own way through school, but seeking financial support from an older married man based on "companionship" seemed very suspect. Lindsey seriously questioned this guy's intentions. But Megan had a point—she was definitely reaping the benefits. Lindsey did the math in her head, and just the tuition alone for a semester was big money, not to mention the gifts and other perks Megan was receiving. If two consenting adults wanted to start this type of relationship, who was she to judge?

Lindsey was curious about the Web sites that Megan referred to, so she opened up her laptop and did a quick Google search. It did not take her long to find a number of "sugar daddy" Web sites. They were basically dating services where older successful men and women could meet young and attractive "goal-oriented" people. Lindsey was disturbed to find that many of the young women demanded allowances that exceeded $3,000 per month for their "companionship." Although sex was never explicitly mentioned, plenty of innuendo in the profile names and pictures indicated that it was definitely something on everyone's mind. Lindsey thought, *So this is the new way to further your career.* The notion of using one's youth and sexuality as a means to garner support seemed cheap and demeaning to Lindsey. She quickly closed her browser and went back to her term paper. They simply would need to agree to disagree on this issue. She would do damage control in the morning.

THE MEDIA'S IMPACT ON POPULAR CULTURE

Culture represents the common customs, traditions, and shared values of a civilization. These customs run deep and are often represented in such things as literature, language, art, music, food, and social habits. The United States is a melting pot of many different cultural influences. Nevertheless, certain shared common cultural values are distinctly American. For example, Americans value independence, freedom, equality, and the belief that anyone can be successful with hard work and commitment. These core values are reflected throughout American culture and thought.

The term *popular culture* refers to societal influences that attain mass appeal and acceptance because they are innovative. These influences often challenge existing cultural and social boundaries, while at the same time establishing new subcultures that unite like-minded individuals. Popular culture relies heavily on the media to reach the masses. Accordingly, the acceptance of popular culture is largely contingent upon its marketability and commercial success. The novelty of popular culture resonates with certain audiences but repulses others.

Popular culture is often criticized as being trendy or irrelevant because it usually has little or no meaningful long-term effect on core cultural values. While this is generally true, popular culture *can* play a significant role in paving the way for sustained social change. Consider Elvis Presley's influence on rock and roll, Michael Jordan's influence on basketball, Run DMC's influence on hip-hop, or Steve Jobs's influence on mobile technology. These are just a few pop cultural icons who were harbingers of significant shifts in society.

Elvis Presley defied social convention by mixing elements of country-western music, gospel music, and rhythm and blues. This fusion of diverse musical styles blurred the lines between music that had been segregated by race. Michael Jordan's incredible skills on the basketball court challenged up-and-coming players to "be like Mike." Moreover, Jordan's endorsement of products—everything from shoes to underwear—set the standard for future lucrative endorsement deals for professional athletes. Run DMC was able to bring hip-hop music and culture into the mainstream. Steve Jobs's ability to reimagine the mobile phone drastically changed the way the world accesses information. These reformers were often dismissed as promulgating passing fads. However, their impact on culture is still felt today and has inspired continued innovation.

Popular culture provides a snapshot of the current trends that are shaping a nation's identity, and it reflects the evolving values of a society.[8] The media plays a significant role in communicating these shared values, which in turn has the potential to change established cultural norms.

ASSESSING THE MEDIA'S EFFECT ON BEHAVIOR

Popular culture and the media have a symbiotic relationship. Popular culture needs media exposure to reach the masses. The media needs a marketable popular culture to attract viewers and pick up sponsors. Individuals who are able to harness the power of the media have tremendous influence over cultural trends.

Given our appetite for uncivil media across multiple platforms, there are concerns that society's increased incivility is directly related to our media consumption. The most recent Civility in America survey found that 55 percent of the people polled expected incivility to worsen in America.[9] People blamed politicians, the news media, celebrities, corporate America, and sports figures for the decline of civility. Interestingly, those who were blamed for making things worse also have the greatest access to mass media.

Is the media merely reflecting an uncivil popular culture that already exists, or has the media created an uncivil popular culture that is putting down roots into American culture at large? Over the years, this issue has been a topic of debate among educators, researchers, and policy makers. The proliferation of incivility in print, music, television, video games, and movies cannot be denied. However, does exposure to incivility through the media *cause* uncivil behavior?

Sex in the Media

Sex sells. If we pick up a magazine, turn on the radio, watch television, or drive down the street, we are likely to be inundated with sounds, images, and messages filled with sexual innuendo. Advertisers use attractive models to promote their products in magazines, in commercials, and on large billboards. Sexual themes are common in popular music. The Internet is a limitless repository of free sex-based media, from Web sites with graphic sexual images to amateur pornography videos. Video games, such as Grand Theft Auto and God of War, often include explicit sex scenes. Americans are exposed to a substantial amount of sexual media across multiple platforms.

The media seems to glorify sex. The messages are generally skewed to reinforce gender stereotypes. Women are portrayed as sexual objects. Women are encouraged to present themselves in provocative ways to attract the attention of men. This includes makeup, perfume, clothing, and the accentuation of certain physical features. Men are encouraged to aggressively pursue women. Masculinity is closely associated with a man's ability to get women into his bedroom. All this occurs behind the backdrop of an exciting party atmosphere where everyone is carefree and having a good time. Noticeably missing from these portrayals are the significant health risks associated with reckless sexual behavior.

What effect, if any, does the onslaught of sex-based media have on our society? Evidence suggests that exposure to sexual media may influence teenagers' attitudes and beliefs about sexual activity. For example, a study conducted by RAND Health found that teens who frequently watched television programs with sexual content are more likely to initiate sexual intercourse within the following year.[10] Repeated exposure to sexual content on television also creates a significantly greater chance of experiencing an unwanted pregnancy. The study also found that heavy exposure to sexually degrading lyrics in music is associated with accelerated initiation of sexual intercourse and other sexual activities.

While a teenager's decision to become sexually active may be an individual choice, it also creates genuine public health concerns. Risky sexual activity among youth can lead to unexpected pregnancies, the spread of sexually transmitted diseases, and sexual assaults. Early sexual activity is also correlated with future substance abuse, truancy, aggression, and behavioral deviance.[11] Premature sexual activity can set a negative trajectory that may be very difficult to change.

The casual manner in which sex is portrayed may influence adolescents' developing views about sex. For example, *sexting*—texting sexually suggestive messages, pictures, or video via mobile phones—is gaining popularity among teens and adults. However, the casualness with which people are willing to send sexual messages, pictures, and videos can have unintended consequences. Once digital pictures and videos are sent, they can take on a life of their own. The intimate pictures can be easily shared without the knowledge of the sender or publicly posted online through social media or YouTube. Sexting is not limited to teens and young adults. Just ask former NFL quarterback Brett Favre and former congressman Anthony Weiner, who had their reputations tarnished by sexting scandals.[12]

While the exact number of teens who engage in sexting is difficult to ascertain, the National Campaign to Prevent Teen and Unplanned Pregnancy estimates that 20 percent of teens have sent nude or seminude pictures or videos of themselves. They also estimate that approximately 39 percent sent sexually suggestive messages without pictures or videos. Sexting typically occurs between persons who are considered to be a boyfriend or a girlfriend, but these messages are also used to establish a hook-up.

A hook-up is another example of the nonchalant attitudes of young people about sexuality. A *hook-up* is a sexual encounter that occurs between people who may range from complete strangers to brief acquaintances or even longtime friends. The hallmark of hooking up is that the encounter has no strings attached. In other words, the hook-up partners usually do not seek a committed relationship, although the same partners may repeatedly hook up over a period of time. In terms of sexual behavior, a hook-up can be just kissing, sexual touching, oral sex, or sexual intercourse.

Some teens and young adults, especially females, view hooking up as the first step to a more committed relationship. While hooking up may develop into some semblance of a more committed relationship, most hook-ups do not. Nevertheless, since hooking up dominates many social scenes—including college campuses—the practice is considered to be the only route to romantic relationships and sexual encounters.

Among young adults, societal attitudes regarding pornography are also shifting. For example, one study of more than eight hundred college students at six universities found that about two-thirds of the men and nearly half of the women surveyed believed viewing pornography is acceptable. This study also posed the same question to the parents of the surveyed students. The results were that only one-third of the fathers and one-fifth of the mothers held the same beliefs as their children regarding the appropriateness of pornography. Approximately 86 percent of the male students surveyed had viewed pornography in the last year, and approximately 20 percent reported viewing pornography daily or at least every other day.[13]

The availability of no-cost pornography online is perhaps one of the biggest contributing factors to the increased acceptance of pornography. One no longer needs to go to an adult bookstore; instead one can access it by using Google on a mobile device. This so-called pocket porn can be accessed anytime and anywhere very discreetly.

Determining whether accessing pornography is civil or uncivil is outside the scope of this book. However, research suggests that excessive use of pornography can have destructive effects.[14] For example, one study found that 56 percent of divorces "involve one party...who has an obsessive interest in pornographic websites." Gail Dines, a professor at Wheelock College in Boston and author of *Pornland: How Porn Has Hijacked Our Sexuality*, noted that pornography often skews attitudes and perceptions about sexuality and women.[15] Dines argues that men who are heavy pornography users begin to construct ideas about sexuality that conform and align with unrealistic fantasies of "the pornographic world." This is often manifested when users of pornography attempt to reenact certain sexual acts that may be violent, demeaning, or degrading to a sexual partner. Other research suggests that pornography use may lead to increased sexual aggression.[16]

Some researchers believe that our heavy saturation of sex-based or sexually suggestive media is changing our attitudes about sexuality. Popular culture, as presented through music, television, movies, and other media sources, has been instrumental in this evolution. This may partly explain Megan's decision to share "companionship" with a much older married man in the opening vignette. Although we do not know whether Megan was having sex with him, all indications were that the relationship was heading that direction. She was clearly using her youth and sexuality as tools to receive financial support. These types of relationships are not new; yet the fact that multiple Web sites unabashedly solicit and promote sugar daddy relationships is another example of a significant cultural shift.

Sex in the media, however, is just one of numerous complex variables that contribute to the changing societal attitudes and cultural norms regarding sex. Other contributing factors include parental supervision, socioeconomic factors, and peer influence.

Notwithstanding youth exposure to sexual media, many of the key public health indicators—such as teen pregnancy and prevalence of sexually transmitted diseases—have dropped significantly. Teen pregnancy rates have continually declined and reached a new record low in 2011.[17] Furthermore, according to the Centers for Disease Control, there have been sharp reductions in the reported cases of many sexually transmitted diseases, including HIV/AIDS.[18] These trends may indicate that while more people view sexuality casually, they understand the risks associated with sexual activity and take appropriate preventive measures.

Violence in the Media

Violence is a major societal concern, especially on high school and college campuses. From Columbine High School to Virginia Tech, we have learned that disturbed students can do the unthinkable. And just when we thought we had hit rock bottom, the tragedy at Sandy Hook Elementary burst into headlines. Adam Lanza shot and killed twenty schoolchildren and six adults at Sandy Hook and then committed suicide.[19] Lanza, who was twenty years old at the time of the shooting, was said to be obsessed with violent video games.[20]

School shootings are not the only manifestation of violence occurring in our society. Bullying plagues students of all ages and is even making its way into the workplace. Sexual violence against women has reached a point where the National Institute of Justice has estimated that about one in five college women will be a victim of sexual assault while at college.[21] College-aged women experience sexual assault at rates four times higher than the assault rate of all other women.

Numerous studies link exposure to violent media to aggressive behavior.[22] This correlation is particularly strong when exposure to media violence occurs at a young age. Some researchers have demonstrated that very young children will imitate aggressive acts they see on television in their play with peers.[23] When children under the age of four are continually exposed to media violence, they may be unable to distinguish between fact and fantasy. Over time children become desensitized and may consider violence as an acceptable form of conflict resolution. This desensitization makes children more aggressive, and this aggression tends to continue into adulthood.[24]

However, exposure to violent media is not the *only* factor contributing to more aggressive behavior. One study found that exposing children to media violence is just one of six risk factors that predict later aggression.[25]

The other five factors include low parental involvement, gender, bias toward hostility, physical victimization, and prior physical fights. The likelihood that a child will display aggressive behavior increases with the number of risk factors associated with the child. According to this study, exposure to media violence is not the biggest indicator for aggressive behavior, but it is the easiest to control.[26]

Adults exposed to violent media may also experience higher rates of aggression, although the effects are largely short-term.[27] For example, one study found that people who played violent video games for three consecutive days showed greater increases in aggressive behavior than those who played nonviolent ones. Dr. Brad Bushman, the coauthor of the study, compared playing violent video games with smoking cigarettes—a single cigarette will not cause lung cancer, but smoking over multiple years greatly increases the risk. According to Bushman, "Repeated exposure to violent video games may have a cumulative effect on aggression."

There seems to be general consensus that violent media in and of itself does not cause people to become more violent and aggressive, but it is a contributing factor. Other complex contributing factors must be assessed, such as an individual's personality, gender, socioeconomic status, and mental health. The amount of media exposure is an important factor. For example, people who are exposed to heavy doses of violent media are more at risk for exhibiting violent behavior. People who have a steady diet of violent media also tend to see the world as a more hostile place, expect others to behave more aggressively, and demonstrate increased levels of aggression.[28]

Although media violence may not be the only cause for the violent aggressive behavior we see, parents, teachers, policy makers, and the media must recognize its potential harms. Over the years the media has responded by creating rating systems to inform the public about content that may be inappropriate for certain audiences. The federal government and some state governments have taken steps to regulate media violence with varying degrees of success. Ultimately, exposure to violent media becomes a personal choice, especially among families with children. An attempt to turn the clock back to the 1950s when violence in the media was almost nonexistent is not feasible and largely unnecessary. As members of a free and democratic society, we must learn to make better choices about the media we consume and know when enough is enough.

Profanity in the Media

In 1939, the movie *Gone with the Wind* shocked audiences when Rhett Butler, played by Clark Gable, uttered the famous line: "Frankly, my dear, I don't give a damn." At that time the use of the word *damn* was considered profane and was not used in reputable films. Following *Gone with the Wind*, profanity has become a staple in movies, television, music, and talk radio. Famous actors, musicians, and athletes casually use profanity in public, on social media, and during interviews and awards programs.

Profanity is not just a staple in the world of entertainment; politicians seem to be incorporating more potty language in their public discourse. From the president of the United States to the local city council, profanity is popping up in interviews, speeches, and even legislative sessions. For example, in the midst of the 2010 BP oil spill in the Gulf of Mexico, President Barack Obama told a reporter in an interview that he was talking with experts to learn enough information to find out "whose ass to kick."[29] In 2004, then Vice President Dick Cheney had a run-in with Senator Patrick Leahy on the Senate floor during a photo session. The conversation famously ended with Cheney telling Leahy to go "f**k yourself." Cheney later jokingly reminisced that his insult to Leahy was "sort of the best thing I ever did."[30] New York Mayor Michael Bloomberg delivered a prepared speech at a hotdog-eating contest during a 2012 Fourth of July celebration on Coney Island. The speech was filled with bad hotdog puns. Bloomberg stopped himself in the middle of the speech and said, "Who wrote this s**t?"

Profanity is also prevalent in the world of business. For example, when Carol Bartz became CEO of Yahoo in January 2009, she reportedly told her staff that if anybody leaked company secrets, she would "drop-kick" them to "f**king Mars." Bartz's propensity for profanity later erupted publicly during a 2010 interview when she told Michael Arrington, founder of TechCrunch, to "f**k off" in response to criticism about her accomplishments at Yahoo.[31]

Sometimes profanity is difficult to avoid. In certain situations it may be the only appropriate response. Imagine for a moment that you accidentally hit your finger with a hammer. Chances are your response will almost reflexively be profane. Now imagine you are properly stopped at a traffic light that is red. You look in your rearview mirror and notice that the driver directly behind you is not paying attention and is about to rear-end your vehicle. The first words that would probably come out of your mouth are not likely to be the most wholesome. While profanity is typically reserved for these types of spontaneous outbursts of anger or shock, it has become fashionable to casually use profanity in everyday conversation.[32]

Casual profanity seems to be part and parcel of the trending decline of decorum and civility in our culture. It is not unusual for people from all walks of life to casually drop f- bombs in restaurants, shopping malls, or other public places where children are around. The casual use of profanity is also frequently used in the workplace among coworkers, outside vendors, and even customers. In higher education, some professors incorporate profanity into their classroom lectures. Although using profanity may be appropriate for the subject matter, in many situations using offensive language has no relationship to the course content.

Clearly, cultural attitudes surrounding the use of profanity have changed since *Gone with the Wind* in 1939. The prevalence of foul language in music, television, movies, and everyday encounters with people in the community has perhaps caused a degree of desensitization. When people are unable to distinguish the difference between appropriate talk for the bathroom and the boardroom, profanity is likely to abound in inappropriate situations. For some people, profanity is a quintessential part of their vernacular.

So what's the big deal? Many people do not see any problem with the casual use of profanity in everyday conversations and, to some extent, in more professional and formal settings. Some celebrities, politicians, and well-known executives believe that this type of gritty rough-around-the-edges style of communicating creates a connection with average people. These high-profile people may use profanity strategically to appear more down-to-earth or ordinary.

While using the occasional expletive for emphasis may be appropriate in certain situations, as members of a larger community, people should be cognizant of their surroundings. How does our choice to use coarse language affect others? Are we truly making connections by using profanity, or are we driving people away? Are there more appropriate ways to communicate a thought or an idea or connect with an audience *without* using profanity? These questions should be used as filters to guide communication with others. In the context of civility, mutual respect toward those around you is paramount. Self-censoring—although it may not be required—is helpful.

CULTURAL SHIFTS

Without a doubt, American culture is changing. It will constantly be in flux as the attitudes and values of American citizens evolve. The media plays a significant role in the changing values of the society. In our efforts to do civility, being mindful of the amount and types of media we consume could be an important factor in improving civility on an individual basis. Taking steps to limit media intake that is disproportionately violent, sexually degrading, obscene, or profane may help our interactions with others.

While many questionable aspects of popular culture are contrary to the notion of civility—mutual respect and community engagement—many cultural shifts should be applauded.

The increased reach of the media provides a greater degree of transparency and a deeper sense of connectivity. Social media allows us to connect virtually with family, friends, and even celebrities. Breaking news and information from around the world—from scientific breakthroughs to politics to the latest Hollywood gossip—are instantly available, complete with robust commentary.

Such transparency and connectivity can be used to perpetuate incivility, but they can also be used to inspire civility. For example, it is amazing to see how Americans can coalesce when confronted with a national tragedy. Americans are quick to support those affected. Celebrities use their influence to bring awareness to an issue and gather public support, musicians host benefit concerts to raise money, large and small corporations make donations in the communities where people are affected, and average citizens volunteer to help out their neighbors in need. Various forms of media are often used to inform the masses and get people involved in the aftermath of catastrophes such as 911, Hurricane Katrina, and Sandy Hook Elementary. We have been able to disregard our differences—culturally and otherwise—and come together as Americans.

TOOLS AND EXERCISES

What Would You Do?

Imagine you are the editor of your school newspaper. One of your journalists is an excellent writer and has consistently produced articles that are both timely and substantive. Recently, she received information about the personal life of the dean of students, who was said to be having an affair with a student. Her source is credible, and she has an excellent history of fact checking. She would like to publish the article. In addition, you just conducted a student survey resulting in feedback outlining readers' general disinterest in the paper and desire for more dynamic material.

1. Do you green-light her article? Explain why or why not.
2. What other options are there for gaining interest and readership for the paper?
3. Do you feel there should be parameters for collegiate student newspapers, or should they remain uncensored? Explain your position.
4. What effects do you think publishing this article will have on the tone and legitimacy of the paper?

The Media Inventory

Make a list of your top two favorite television shows, video games, magazines, books, and Web sites. What does each say about you and your interests? How would you describe them in terms of civility: language, sexual content, violence, gossip, substance, political activism, involvement, and so on?

*I've often said that the top's cheating to thrive,
the bottom's cheating to survive, and those in
the middle are content with their grades and
just go along in life and are happy.*
— **Professor Donald McCabe**

CHAPTER 4

Student Classroom Incivility

It probably comes as no surprise that many professors complain of a marked increase in student incivility in the classroom. Student classroom conduct merely reflects the uncivil cultural norms in our society. Student behaviors toward professors and other students are influenced by complex forces such as life experiences, political affiliation, and to some degree pop culture. In a sense, the classroom has become a microcosm of our society.

Cheating and plagiarism are forms of student incivility frequently occurring in the classroom. Cheating occurs when students use deceptive practices to gain unfair advantage on projects, quizzes, or exams. Cheaters are able to game the academic system by relying on prohibited external information to complete course requirements rather than demonstrating a mastery of the course content.

When students take credit for academic work actually done by another, they are engaging in plagiarism. Students plagiarize by copying information found online or in print without providing proper citation or by collaborating with other students on individual projects. Students who plagiarize misappropriate the work and ideas of others and then present them as their own.

Cheating and plagiarism circumvent the learning process and misrepresent student attainment. Students who cheat and plagiarize are effectively stealing another's work and then lying about its source. Although most students understand that cheating and plagiarism are wrong, they may be confused about academic standards and requirements. Professors also commonly express annoyance about students disrupting class. Some students aggressively challenge a professor's authority, ability to teach, and grading policies.

This chapter addresses how student classroom incivility can interfere with student learning, growth, and development. When student behavior violates principles of academic integrity or disrupts the class, it triggers incivility. This type of uncivil conduct represents a complete disregard for the instructors and the other students who are attempting to learn course content. While most students are civil in the classroom, it takes only a few bad apples to disrupt the entire class. This chapter discusses ways colleges and universities can promote greater civility among students and encourage students to do civility.

ONLINE CHEATING: JACOB

As Jacob was considering the classes he would take during the fall semester, signing up for at least one online course seemed logical. The freedom associated with completing course work on his own schedule was way too attractive to pass up. The university was offering Intro to American Studies, which at the time seemed like a relatively low-maintenance, straightforward, and easy course. With one less class to attend during the week, his schedule would be open to the most important aspect of college life—socializing!

Jacob pitched his idea to his friends on Facebook. He posted, "Thinking about taking Intro to American Studies online. Should be EASY! Who's in?"

Besides getting forty-seven "likes," Jacob was able to persuade two of his friends—Mark and Adam—to enroll in the online course with him. The three friends were stoked! They agreed to work together on course assignments. It would be even *easier* since they would be collaborating.

The old saying, "the best-laid plans of mice and men often go awry," was playing out for Jacob and his friends. Once the fall semester was in full swing, they quickly discovered that the online course was not as easy as they initially assumed. In addition to reading assignments, quizzes, and a final exam, students were graded on class participation. This required students to post comments and questions to an online discussion board based on course content at least twice a week.

Although Jacob and his friends had loosely agreed to work together on course materials, it never happened. For Jacob, keeping up with the online course became increasingly difficult. The demands of other classes, hanging out with his friends, and his budding relationship with Abby did not leave much extra time for his online class. Four weeks into the semester, there were times he had almost forgotten he was enrolled in the class.

One night, when Jacob and Mark were enjoying a lazy night playing video games on the Xbox, Jacob received a text from Adam. The game of choice was *Need for Speed: Most Wanted.* While trying to outrun and maneuver a digital cop in the game, Jacob attempted to simultaneously read the text message on his iPhone. With one eye on the game and the other on his iPhone, Jacob read the message: "Hey, man. Ready for the Intro to American Studies quiz tomorrow?"

Jacob's heart dropped to his feet as his Porsche 911 collided head-on with an SUV and spun out of control.

Mark yelled, "C'mon man! What was that? You got to keep your eyes on the road! Tell Abby to leave you alone while you are running from the law!"

Jacob replied half in a panic, "That wasn't Abby. It was Adam. He said there's a quiz tomorrow in American Studies!"

"Okay. So, what are you worried about?" Mark replied.

Jacob retorted, "I don't have a clue what's going on in that class! I'm not even sure I remember how to log in!"

"Get a grip, man," Mark said. "Remember the plan— *collaboration*! Look, the quiz is online right?"

"Yes. So what's your point?" Jacob said.

"My point is that we work *together* on the quiz. Three heads are better than one! Text Adam and see if he can meet with us tomorrow to take the quiz. Here's what we'll do. You start the quiz and tell us the questions. I'll Google each question for the answer. Adam can scan the book for additional pertinent information. No one will ever know. It's foolproof!"

Jacob thought momentarily about Mark's proposition. While he wanted to work together with Mark and Adam on the course, he did not think it would come to this. It was clear that if he took the quiz based on his current competence of the subject matter, he was likely to fail. Plus his lack of class participation was already a strike against his final grade. Collaborating on the quiz seemed to be the only solution.

However, Jacob was reluctant to agree to Mark's scheme. Jacob had already had a run-in with the university's Honor Council during his freshman year. Jacob's world history professor had reported him to the Honor Council for failing to cite facts properly in a research paper. The whole process was incredibly distressing. A violation of the university's academic integrity policy could result in an academic dismissal. Yet Jacob emerged from the process with basically a slap on the wrist and made a personal commitment never to be in that situation again.

"What's wrong?" Mark asked inquisitively. "Text Adam. We got this one!"

Jacob did not feel right. Working together on the quiz seemed more like cheating than collaborating. He seemed trapped.

CHEATING IN THE CLASSROOM

Incivility often manifests itself in the classroom in the form of cheating—especially on exams. There are infinite ways that students can cheat. Let's just say there are lots of imaginative students. Cheating can be as low-tech as using a pen to tattoo notes on body parts or as high-tech and innovative as using the approach of Jacob and his friends.

In addition to the imaginative cheaters, there are the very sophisticated cheaters who game the system by capitalizing on new and unique technology and methods to cheat. For example, in 2013, two students at Miami University in Oxford, Ohio, discovered a way to hack into the university's computerized grading system unnoticed and change their grades and the grades of more than fifty other students. The student hackers installed a key logger—a commonly used surveillance software—on several of their professors' computers. Using this software, the students were able to capture usernames and passwords to get full access to the university's grading system and other unauthorized information such as midterms and final exams. The student hackers operated covertly without being detected over a two-year period.[1] The scheme was ultimately foiled when one of their professors noticed a discrepancy between her paper grade sheet and the grades posted online.[2] Both students were ultimately dismissed from the university and faced criminal charges.[3]

In 2011, five high school students in Nassau County, New York, were found to have impersonated other high school students during ACT and SAT examinations. One of the five teenagers implicated in the scheme had actually taken tests for girls with gender-neutral names—including his girlfriend—and had created fake identification. Fifteen students were found to have paid these impersonators as much as $3,600 to take the test as their proxy.[4]

According to an extensive four-year survey of 14,000 undergraduate students conducted by Donald McCabe, two-thirds of students admitted to cheating on tests, homework, and assignments.[5] Research shows that while cheating occurs among students of all levels, students at the top and bottom tend to cheat the most. According to McCabe, "The top's cheating to thrive, the bottom's cheating to survive."[6]

David Callahan, author of *The Cheating Culture*, suggests student cheating is related to the widespread cheating culture observed in all aspects of American life, including business, sports, and academia. Callahan points to a "winner take all society," in which the rewards for being the best can be so great that students will do whatever it takes to win.[7] The payoffs of cheating are too great to ignore.

Researchers believe that students are seduced into cheating for various reasons. One of the main drivers is the intense academic pressure that some students put on themselves to succeed. Competition to get into good universities and graduate schools is fierce. Admission into top schools is often seen as a ticket to future success, and many highly motivated students will do whatever it takes to get in—even if it means bending the rules.

Often academic pressure is intensified by student over commitment. When other classes, jobs, and social commitments consume the student's time, the workload can become unmanageable. Cheating is seen as an escape. Research shows that "panic cheating" or "cheating under duress" increases when a student has a low grade point average or is under pressure to maintain a scholarship.[8]

Another factor contributing to student cheating is perceived leniency in enforcing academic integrity policies. Most students who cheat rarely get caught, and those who are caught receive just a mild reprimand.[9] Faculty members who suspect students may be cheating are often reluctant to report. A variety of factors contribute to this reluctance—especially the burden of carrying out cumbersome hearing procedures.[10] If students notice their colleagues are getting away with cheating, the legitimacy of the system is compromised, and students are more likely to view cheating as justified.

Students may interpret leniency in taking proactive steps to prevent cheating as an implicit statement by the university that academic integrity is not all that important. When institutions turn a blind eye to violations of academic integrity or fail to stress the imperative of honesty in the examination process, students may view this almost as an invitation to cheat. It is clear the institution's attitude toward academic integrity can set the tone for the student body and either foster or constrain the cheating culture.

Interestingly, as Jacob considered collaborating with his friend on the online quiz, he recalled his last encounter with the university's Honor Council. The council's tepid response made him seriously reconsider bending the rules again. Jacob may be willing to gamble that he won't get caught cheating on the quiz, and if he was to get caught, the university's response would be another slap on the wrist. However, with another strike against him, the Honor Council may not be as forgiving.

Peer acceptance of cheating is also another contributing factor. According to David Rettinger, a cognitive psychologist at the University of Mary Washington, even when students know cheating is against the rules "most still look to their peers for cues as to what behaviors and attitudes are acceptable."[11] One study found that students whose peers regularly cheat or whose peers consider cheating to be an acceptable practice are also more likely to engage in academic misconduct.[12]

The belief that everyone is cheating creates a social norm among students that academic dishonesty is just a part of college life.[13] This social norm of cheating may encourage students who might not otherwise cheat to do so just to stay competitive, especially when so many cheaters seem to get away with it.

Students typically don't start cheating when they arrive on campus. Most cheating begins in high school. A study by the Josephson Institute of Ethics of 40,000 high school students found that more than half of teenage students cheated on a test during the last school year, and one third admitted to using the Internet to plagiarize an assignment.[14]

Typically, cheating does not stop when students leave academia. Research suggests that academic cheating continues with other forms of dishonesty later in life, such as breaking workplace rules, cheating on spouses, or lying to a customer. Students who habitually cheat stop viewing their conduct as immoral. Consequently, taking steps to curb academic dishonesty and creating new community norms about cheating are crucial to educating responsible and civil adults.

The way cheating has been trivialized by students demonstrates a disregard for core academic values and also a lack of civility. Cheating circumvents the learning process, skews academic measurement, and results in a misleading representation of actual attainment. Engaging in cheating also demonstrates disrespect for other students who actually work hard to achieve, professors who attempt to engage students in learning, and the academic community that strives for excellence.

PLAGIARISM

Of the many forms of academic misconduct, plagiarism is probably the most common. *Plagiarism* is defined as "the deliberate and knowing presentation of another person's original ideas or creative expressions as one's own."[15] In its most basic sense, plagiarism is the verbatim copying—or cutting and pasting—of someone else's words without acknowledging the original author through use of quotation marks and proper citation. However, it can also be defined more broadly to include paraphrasing another author's work or borrowing someone else's original ideas without proper attribution. Thus, work that was produced in collaboration with other students could also be termed *plagiarism* when a professor has explicitly prohibited such cooperation.

Harvard gained international attention in 2012 when 125 students taking an introductory government course were accused of plagiarism on a take-home final exam.[16] The final exam was open book, open note, and open Internet. The only restriction was that students were not allowed to work together on the exam.

The accused students allegedly plagiarized by working together in groups of varying sizes and sharing answers. After an investigation, more than half of the students were ordered to withdraw from the school for a period of time.[17] Two of the students implicated in the scandal were stars on the men's basketball team. Both student athletes voluntarily withdrew, missing the entire 2012–2013 basketball season.[18] Of the remaining students, approximately half were placed on disciplinary probation, and the rest were dismissed.

A growing body of research demonstrates that plagiarism is on the rise in American colleges and universities.[19] Colleges and universities across America and even around the world are seeing similar increases in academic dishonesty. Many attribute the rise in plagiarism to the pervasive use of electronic research where, with a click of a mouse, content can be easily cut and pasted into assignments and papers without proper citation.[20]

Research from the Center for Academic Integrity shows that 77 percent of students did not believe that cut-and-paste plagiarism was a serious issue.[21] Many students regard plagiarism as a matter of academic etiquette that should be avoided simply to escape punishment.[22] The perceived victimless nature of plagiarism may be one reason that students do not consider it a serious issue. If plagiarism is nothing more than impolite academic behavior, there is no real reason to avoid it other than to minimize the risk of punishment.

Perhaps another contributor to the surge in plagiarism is a lack of education—students do not understand what plagiarism encompasses. Complicating matters is that proper citation may vary by discipline and even among different professors. Communication can be one of the most effective methods of preventing plagiarism, particularly plagiarism resulting from improper citation. To reduce the confusion that can exist about proper citations, institutions may encourage faculty to adopt recognized writing styles, such as the Modern Language Association (MLA) style, *Chicago Manual of Style*, or American Psychological Association (APA) style.

When professors take the time to educate and inform students about plagiarism within the context of an assignment, they may be able to prevent unintentional acts of academic dishonesty. Just putting the university's plagiarism policy in the course syllabus is not enough to prevent plagiarism, nor can it account for the range of nuanced requirements that differ among writing styles, instructors, and disciplines.

While some instances of plagiarism are unintentional, many students plagiarize deliberately. They intentionally turn in someone else's work, cut and paste large sections of information from the Internet without using quotation marks or citing a source, and improperly collaborate on projects and assignments. The root cause of this type of plagiarism is laziness.

New tools are available to help instructors detect plagiarism. For example, Turnitin.com is a Web-based system that scans student papers against 4.5 billion pages of books and journals and millions of documents already submitted through the system.[23] The system produces an originality report within minutes of submission that instructors can use to identify instances of deliberate plagiarism.

In addition, some professors are taking low-tech measures to combat plagiarism, such as requiring some sources to have been published within the past year or to be from a prepared list. Instructors may set several intermediate deadlines along the way. If the student has to submit a topic proposal, preliminary research report, and rough draft before the final paper is due, it is less likely that the student will be able to procrastinate and pull something off the Internet at the last minute. Additionally, requiring an annotated bibliography—in which the student must identify the source and where it was obtained and must reflect briefly on its applicability and reliability—ensures that the student will do independent research.

DISRUPTIVE STUDENTS

Perhaps the most visible manifestation of student incivility in the classroom is disruptive students. Teaching cannot be effective in a classroom where there are frequent problems with decorum and civility. When a teacher is unable to encourage student engagement in the classroom due to frequent student disruptions, student grades and learning are adversely affected.[24] Disruptive students can undermine a class's educational value by constantly distracting the instructor and other students.[25] Such conduct represents a lack of mutual respect of others and a disregard for the classroom community.

Uncivil disruptive students are not a new phenomenon. The struggle over appropriate classroom behavior in higher education has been around for hundreds of years. For example, as early as the thirteenth century, the bishop in the Episcopal Court of Paris described his students the following way: "They attend class but make no effort to learn anything."[26] During this period, there were recorded instances at other European universities of students who physically attacked professors over their grades.[27]

Today, professors commonly complain that students disrupt class by carrying on running conversations, surfing the Internet, texting, eating, and playing on their mobile devices.[28] Some students may aggressively challenge a professor's authority, ability to teach, and grading policies. This type of conduct is disruptive and diversionary and reduces student engagement.

While most students respect the decorum of the classroom, it takes only one person to disrupt the entire class. When students continue to act out in class, they miss valuable learning opportunities and interfere with the learning of other students. Research suggests that there is a direct correlation between classroom disruptions and student learning.[29] Uncivil classroom conduct is also linked to students leaving the institution before graduation. If the classroom environment is not conducive to learning, students may choose to transfer to another institution.

Disruptive student behavior generally falls into four categories—annoyances, classroom terrorism, intimidation, and threats or attacks.[30]

Annoyances

Annoyances are probably the most common forms of student distractions.[31] For example, annoyances occur when students arrive late or leave early, allow their mobile phones to ring during a lecture, or noisily pack up before class has dismissed. Annoying students are completely oblivious to others and typically do not recognize the disruptive effect they have on the instructor or the class. Yet their conduct, if it persists, can change the classroom dynamic for the worse.

Class size is often an important factor when dealing with annoying student behavior. Larger classes tend to provide more opportunities for student disruptions. Larger classes create an "anonymous atmosphere where students are more likely to engage in uncivil behavior."[32] The anonymity and impersonal nature of a large class can inspire students to behave in ways they would never dream of exhibiting in small classes. Small classes allow professors to know everyone's name and provide more one-on-one opportunities with students.

Many annoying student disruptions can be managed by establishing clear classroom norms during the first week of class.[33] Setting clear behavioral expectations at the onset helps students better understand their responsibilities—both as individuals and as members of the classroom community. The goal is to facilitate a classroom environment that promotes student engagement and learning.

Most Uncivil Classroom Behaviors [34]

1. Talking After Being Asked to Stop
2. Coming to Class Under the Influence
3. Allowing a Cellphone to Ring
4. Nonverbally Showing Disrespect
5. Swearing
6. Sleeping
7. Making Disparaging Remarks
8. Arriving Late/Leaving Early
9. Texting
10. Packing Up Books Before Class Is Over
11. Using Electronic Devices for Non-Class Activities

Classroom Terrorists

Classroom terrorists refer to students who monopolize class time with personal agendas. They often ask irrelevant questions, derailing the professor with unnecessary rabbit trails. While these students may be engaged, their classroom involvement effectively holds everyone else hostage. When classroom terrorists are able to dominate classroom discussions, other students disengage. When students check out, learning outcomes decrease.

As with other forms of student disruptions, classroom terrorists may not intend to distract. These students are very enthusiastic about course content—perhaps overly enthusiastic. Nevertheless, if the students are not kept in check, they can suck the life and energy out of a classroom discussion.

Intimidation

Student intimidation is another form of disruptive student behavior occurring in the classroom. Students may threaten to report their professor to the administration or give a negative evaluation to pressure the instructor to succumb to student demands. These tactics can be a major annoyance for professors. If a student submits a complaint against a professor, the complaint might be placed in the professor's employment file, or an informal investigation might be conducted by a department chair or dean. These frivolous student complaints could potentially have a negative effect on a professor's promotion or contract renewal.

Students increasingly view their education through a consumer perspective. In their eyes, getting a degree is much like purchasing an expensive pair of shoes. The student customer pays tuition to the institution to obtain a degree.[35] Professors are viewed more as customer service representatives rather than experts in their fields of study. This consumer mentality may explain why some students are disrespectful and disruptive in class.[36] After all, they paid their tuition; therefore, they can come and go as they please, talk when they want, or even challenge the professor's authority and then demand an A.

Some disgruntled students have upped the ante with intimidation. Rather than report the professors to a department chair or dean, they seek judicial redress from the courts. Recently, Megan Thode, a graduate student at Lehigh University, sued her professors over a C+ she received in an internship. Thode alleged that her mediocre grade kept her from getting her degree and becoming a licensed therapist. The lawsuit demanded the professor change her grade and sought to recover $1.3 million, allegedly the value of a master's degree in counseling psychology.[37] This is not the first student lawsuit over a subpar grade.

Threats or Attacks

Threats or attacks are the most serious form of student disruption. While this type of distraction rarely occurs, it does happen. Professors typically receive violent threats from angry students over grades. These threats can occur in the classroom, but they increasingly occur through e-mail and social media. For example, in 2008, a Penn State student sent a series of threatening e-mails to his professor over a B- he received in a course.[38] According to a press release, the student's e-mail read, "I swear to God I am going to [expletive] put you in a wheelchair when I see you."[39] The professor gave the threatening e-mail to the police, and the student was ultimately arrested.

Sometimes the violence comes without warning. For example, in 2005, Mary Elizabeth Hooker, an associate professor of clinical laboratory and nutritional sciences, was stabbed and beaten by a student over a failing grade.[40] According to the police reports, the student followed Hooker home and stabbed her, slashed her neck, ripped off her shirt, and beat her.

The student was apprehended by the police and charged with assault with intent to murder.[41]

When a student threatens or physically attacks another student or a professor, campus security should be contacted immediately. Anticipating when a student might be a potential threat is problematic, however. Greg Boles, a global manager at the risk management firm Kroll, told *Inside Higher Education*, "Students who try to attack professors generally do provide 'warning signs' but they aren't always identified until after an assault."[42] Sometimes students will comment to a friend or another faculty member about their intention to attack, but these comments are often not taken seriously. Boles recommends that colleges and universities establish a phone number where members of the campus community can report threatening conduct anonymously. According to Boles, people are often embarrassed to report their fears to campus officials.[43]

PROMOTING CIVILITY IN THE CLASSROOM

While it is difficult to control student behavior, professors can employ strategies to promote a more civil and engaging environment. Professors must be proactive, realizing that student disruptions are inevitable. Ignoring the problem will not make it go away. In fact, it could make things worse for everyone. Taking early steps to reduce disruptions can maximize student engagement and learning outcomes for the entire class.

Initially, faculty should establish clear classroom expectations with regard to behavior. Doing this may seem a bit juvenile for the college level, but students may truly be oblivious to proper classroom decorum. Behavioral expectations can be included in the course syllabus and Web page. However these standards are communicated, the professor should discuss the issue of classroom decorum with the class. By discussing classroom behavioral expectations early, the professor eliminates ambiguity regarding appropriate classroom conduct.

If students are disruptive, the professor should immediately address the conduct. Inconsistencies in dealing with rude or disrespectful behavior could send the message to students that classroom civility is not taken seriously. Equally important, the professor must model civil conduct in class.

TOOLS AND EXERCISES

Perspectives

All of us view situations from our own vantage points. Students, instructors, and administrators interact to create the culture of a particular institution. But each of these groups has its unique perspectives on civility. The following questions are meant to prompt discussion among these groups. Find a fellow student and one professor or administrator to interview, and pose these questions to them. How are their answers different and/or similar? Do you see things differently after hearing their responses? How could you bridge the divide between opinions that differ?

1. What is the point of an institutional civility policy if disciplinary action cannot be taken?
2. If most students who cheat rarely get caught, how does an institution promote honesty?
3. How should students be held accountable for cheating or plagiarism?
4. Is plagiarism a victimless crime?
5. How could student viewpoints be incorporated into disciplinary decisions, i.e., peer-review boards?
6. Some schools encourage self-grading or peer-grading. What would be some pros and cons associated with this type of evaluation?
7. How would you handle a classroom terrorist?

Alternative to Cheating

Consider Jacob's dilemma at the beginning of the chapter. Jacob had to choose whether to cheat on an online exam with his two friends. If Jacob asked you for advice, what would you tell him? List three alternatives to cheating.

Explain Your Advice to Jacob:

_____

_____

_____

List Three Alternatives to Cheating:

1.

2.

3.

A person is a person through other people.
—**Nontombi Naomi Tutu**

CHAPTER 5

Uncivil Professors

Professors are learned experts who are charged with seeking truth through rigorous research, study, and inquiry. In turn, they guide student learning, discuss their research and ideas with colleagues, and seek to serve the community based on their expertise. They are critically important members of the higher education community. When professorial conduct becomes uncivil—lacking mutual respect and concern for the community—the entire campus suffers.

Professorial incivility typically falls into three general categories: (1) disrespect and lack of collegiality toward colleagues; (2) disrespect toward students; and (3) academic misconduct. Uncivil conduct can have profound effects on faculty cohesiveness and productivity, student learning, and the reputation of an entire institution.

Addressing faculty incivility—often nuanced or unintended—can be challenging. Honest contention over research and ideas can trigger vigorous debate among members of the academic community, which is a healthy development. Vetting ideas is crucial to learning. However, the

71

vetting process can sometimes deteriorate into inappropriate personal attacks. Distinguishing between honest critique and uncivil discourse can be problematic. At times attempts to address faculty incivility can be construed as an attack on academic freedom.

This chapter analyzes how professorial incivility can impair professional relationships with colleagues, hinder student learning, and violate professional standards of conduct.

POWER STRUGGLES IN THE DEPARTMENT: LINDSEY

Lindsey was ecstatic when she learned that she was able to get into Dr. Mathew Melton's Civil War and Reconstruction course during the fall semester. Although Lindsey was a history major, the course she took during her freshman year almost made her change her major. She had unfortunately caught the ire of Professor Alan Simpson after he discovered she espoused some moderately conservative views. He regularly ridiculed Lindsey in class and, in Lindsey's view, graded her papers lower when she took positions that were contrary to his left-of-center perspectives.

Although she passed the course with a B–, it was the lowest grade she had *ever* received in her entire academic career. Lindsey was convinced that her ideological differences with Professor Simpson affected her final grade and destroyed her perfect 4.0 GPA.

Determined *never* to take another course with Simpson, Lindsey did her due diligence when registering for fall classes her sophomore year. She went to RateMyProfessors.com and saw that Dr. Melton had very high student ratings and tons of positive reviews. Almost everyone Lindsey had spoken to had positive things to say about him—or "Dr. M&M" as he was referred to around campus.

Melton was a young adjunct professor who taught various courses in the History Department. He had an excellent reputation on campus as having solid academic credentials and being a down-to-earth instructor. He was a prolific history blogger and recently had an article published in the *Journal of American History* on the weaponry and technology used in the Civil War. He also hosted a weekly informal community history discussion at a pub located just outside the campus called The Well. Interactive and engaging, the discussions examined current events from a historical perspective. These Well discussions as they became known were often attended by university students.

However, Melton's popularity was not celebrated by everyone, especially among a small group of high-ranking tenured professors in the History Department. Professor Simpson was his chief critic. Simpson was not impressed with Melton's high student evaluations. He surmised that the positive evaluations were the result of Melton's placating students. Simpson sneered at Melton's history blog as bastardized research. In his mind blogging was inappropriate for *true* academic work. Although Melton held a Ph.D. from a respectable state university, Simpson rarely acknowledged Melton as a peer and took steps whenever possible to exclude Melton from faculty planning meetings and social events.

When a new tenure track position opened, Professor Simpson was stunned to learn that the associate dean and the department chair were considering Dr. Melton for the position. Professor Simpson decided it was time to talk with Dean Angela Buckingham.

Professor Simpson knocked on the half-opened door of Dean Buckingham's office.

"Well, come in, Dr. Simpson," said Dean Buckingham. She was a bit surprised by his appearance and tried to remain pleasant despite the fact that she knew the only time Professor Simpson came around was when he had a problem.

"Do you have a moment to talk?" asked Professor Simpson.

"Sure. What's on your mind?"

Simpson wasted no time, going straight to the issue, "I understand Matt is being considered for the new tenure track position."

"That's correct," said Dean Buckingham. "Dr. Melton has done an exceptional job during his last three years as an adjunct lecturer. We feel his quality of teaching, community service, and dedication to research are exactly what our growing History Department needs."

Professor Simpson took a deep breath and said, "Look, Dean. Matt is a good kid. He's bright and students love him. But we have a nationally recognized program here. I think we could do better than a wannabe academic blogger who teaches part-time."

Dean Buckingham was slightly shocked and irritated by Professor Simpson's stinging characterization. She replied, "You do realize Dr. Melton recently had an article published in the *Journal of American History*. The article was excellent. It has put him and our History Department in a very good light. By the way, when was the last time you published something, Dr. Simpson?"

Dean Buckingham's last question made Simpson realize his influence in the department was beginning to wane. He had been loosely working on a book for the last several years on race relations in the Obama era; at this point it was nothing more than an outline.

"I have not published anything of late," replied Professor Simpson, "but my book is coming along nicely. Thanks for asking."

"Wonderful," replied Dean Buckingham in a slightly sarcastic tone, "I look forward to reading it."

Simpson realized he could not attack Melton's academic credentials, so he decided to change tactics. He had one last trick up his sleeve that he did not want to use, but desperate times call for desperate measures.

"Look, Dean," Simpson said frankly, "I trust your judgment on this, but I'm just a little concerned that Matt might be a little *too* close to students."

"What do you mean?" Dean Buckingham inquired.

"Matt holds a weekly history talk at The Well that attracts a lot of our students."

"You mean the bar?" asked Dean Buckingham.

"Yes, the bar," Simpson said indignantly. He knew he had struck a nerve and went for the kill. "Our students simply don't need any more excuses to consume alcohol! By encouraging students to attend these so called history discussions, Matt is blurring the line regarding appropriate professional conduct with students, not to mention violating university policy. He's basically condoning alcohol consumption for many of his students who are under the legal drinking age."

Dean Buckingham's face turned white. After a moment of awkward silence, she replied, "This is not good. Not good at all."

Professor Simpson thought, *Checkmate!*

It did not take the administration long to confirm that Melton was conducting history discussions in a pub that attracted students. His adjunct teaching appointment was immediately terminated without any warning or investigation about whether his conduct violated university policy.

Lindsey could not believe her eyes. She was quickly checking her e-mail on her phone while waiting outside Starbucks to meet a friend for coffee when she noticed an official message from the university with the subject line "Schedule Change Civil War & Recon." She immediately opened the message and read the first few lines:

> *Dear Student,*
>
> *Dr. Mathew Melton is no longer working for the university. Civil War and Reconstruction will be taught this semester by Professor Alan Simpson. Please check the Web site for an updated syllabus. . . .*

Lindsey could not bear to read any more. One thing was certain. She was definitely dropping Professor Simpson's course and possibly changing her major.

DISRESPECT AND LACK OF COLLEGIALITY

Professor Simpson vividly demonstrated how incivility and strife between colleagues in an academic department can be miserable for everyone. Simpson's inflated opinion of himself, desire to wield power, and jealousy most likely deepened existing schisms between adjuncts and tenured faculty within the department. His conduct also sabotaged Dr. Melton's career and may have caused other students, such as Lindsey, to reconsider their majors—perhaps even transfer to another institution.

When professors see themselves as deserving of service, attention, and recognition rather than serving others, they can become islands unto themselves. This can be a very lonely place. Self-absorbed professors let their egos prevent them from helping students, serving in their departments, or mentoring younger colleagues. Like crabs in a bucket, they are constantly pulling others down to advance themselves. The end result is that everyone suffers, including students.

Imagine what would have happened if Professor Simpson had attempted to build a professional relationship with Dr. Melton rather than tear him down. The relationship could have been mutually beneficial. Professor Simpson could have gained some insight from the younger adjunct about publishing, engaging students, and using technology in the classroom. Professor Simpson could have incorporated Dr. Melton into his research and writing on race relations in the Obama era. The two could have established a valuable coauthor relationship that would have propelled Professor Simpson's name back into academic circles and provided an inroad for Dr. Melton to advance his career. Clearly, Dr. Melton would have benefited from having an older, tenured professor showing him the ropes. For example, Professor Simpson could have warned Dr. Melton about the potential conflicts with university policy and his discussions at the local pub that attracted students.

Professors Simpson's conduct also demonstrated a lack of collegiality. *Collegiality* has become a buzzword among faculty members, although the term's definition and application are a bit ambiguous. Generally, *collegiality* refers to a professor's ability to work constructively with colleagues and demonstrate good academic citizenship. This may include sharing the load and contributing fairly to teaching, committee assignments, admission processes, and other academic responsibilities. Collegiality does not mean that a professor must become a yes-man or ignore personal convictions to go along with the crowd. However, it does mean that professors express their differences in a civil and respectful manner. Many colleges and universities have begun citing collegiality with increasing frequency as a factor in making employment decisions, and courts have consistently upheld these decisions.[1]

Most would agree that collegiality, along with civility and respect, vitally affects the performance of professors and enhances their relationships with colleagues and students. A professor's ability to interact and cooperate with colleagues and students has a significant influence on the professor's performance as a teacher and scholar.

Lacking collegiality, departments can develop factions of teachers who do not cooperate and are unable to work together professionally. Fractious relationships can become so serious at times that they develop into significant riffs on important issues such as curriculum and program philosophy. These differences, left unchecked, can cause serious harm to the department, its faculty, and its students. The differences can also stymie departmental decisions and objectives.

Incivility is also an issue among professors when there is disagreement on research, ideas, and theories. Critiques of others' research and ideas can sometimes degenerate into unnecessary and unprofessional personal attacks on colleagues and other nefarious conduct. For example, Tihomir Petrov, an assistant professor at California State University Northridge, was caught by a surveillance camera urinating on a colleague's office door following a dispute with a colleague within his department. Such conduct was not just uncivil and ridiculous; it was illegal. Petrov was charged with two misdemeanors.[2]

According to the American Association of University Professors' (AAUP's) Statement of Professional Ethics, professors have a professional obligation to "respect and defend the free inquiry of associates, even when it leads to findings and conclusions that differ from their own."[3] In other words, urinating on a colleague's door in response to an ideological disagreement will not fly. The notion of extending respect to colleagues who hold divergent views is consistent with the first element of our working definition of civility—mutual respect. However, mutual respect is often counterintuitive, especially when a colleague espouses repugnant views. Professors may take truth seeking to the extreme and attack or denigrate those who see things differently. The line between honest critique and professional insult can be razor thin.

Additionally, the AAUP's Statement of Professional Ethics is clear that professors must "accept their share of faculty responsibilities for the governance of their institution."[4] This statement points directly to community service, the second element in our working definition of civility. Service within the academic department and service on the campus are quintessential elements of faculty on campus.

INCIVILITY TOWARD STUDENTS

The student-professor relationship can be intensely intimate. In certain circumstances a professor may wield substantial influence and control over students. This is particularly true when a professor's course, grade, or recommendation is viewed by students as necessary to enter graduate school or to further their careers. Highly motivated students may become even more vulnerable to professorial abuse.

While most professors are committed to free discussion and open inquiry during lectures, students perceive that some professors are using the classrooms as platforms for political and social indoctrination. Clearly, professors are permitted to have opinions on sociopolitical issues and express these views in class, especially when they are germane to the curriculum. However, when these views result in pedagogical narrowness or are inserted into classroom discussions that bear no relationship to the content of the class, the conduct becomes more problematic.

Professors often rely on their right to academic freedom to justify their conduct in the classroom. Faculty academic freedom typically includes the right to study, discuss, investigate, teach, and publish without institutional interference. At public colleges and universities, academic freedom is a constitutional right, closely associated as a by-product of the First Amendment.[5] At private institutions, academic freedom is generally a contractual right.[6] However, students also have rights in the classroom. For example, they should not be subjected to a hostile learning environment or unfair assessment based on their ideas, beliefs, and political affiliations.

Conduct by professors that is brash, personally demeaning, and retaliatory is not covered under faculty academic freedom protections. Courts have consistently found that academic freedom does not give faculty members a blank check to say or do whatever they want in the classroom. Specifically, academic freedom does not mean that faculty members can harass, threaten, intimidate, ridicule, or impose their views on students.[7] Any conduct by a professor that creates a hostile learning environment or compromises a student's right to learn is not likely to be covered by academic freedom.[8]

In 2007, the AAUP released a report titled "Freedom in the Classroom," which provides professional guidance on how professors should interact with students during classroom discussion. The report noted contemporary criticism by professors abusing the classroom to indoctrinate rather than educate. This includes a failure of professors to represent fairly conflicting views on contentious subjects, intolerance of students' religious, political, and socioeconomic views, and interjection of political and ideological material that is irrelevant to the subject of instruction.[9]

The AAUP report affirms that teachers are "entitled to freedom in the classroom in discussing their subject." However, these freedoms must be balanced in an "atmosphere that is respectful and welcoming to all persons." According to the report, professors breach professional ethics if they "hold up a student to obloquy or ridicule in class" for advancing an idea grounded in religion, politics, or anything else.[10] This does not mean that a professor should not challenge a student's ideas during class. The issue of professionalism and civility centers on how the professor responds to students who make reasoned objections to course material.

In 2005, the American Council on Education (ACE), along with twenty-seven other higher education organizations, released a joint "Statement on Academic Rights and Responsibilities." The statement addresses concerns regarding intellectual pluralism and academic freedom in higher education. The statement avoids attempting to legislate "a single definition or set of standards," noting that faculty and student rights and responsibilities will vary based on each institution's academic mission. Nevertheless, the statement identifies several "overarching principles." The joint statement concludes that higher education institutions should welcome "intellectual pluralism and the free exchange of ideas," and discussions should be "held in an environment characterized by openness, tolerance, and civility."[11] This means that students should have the right to express divergent views in a nonhostile environment.

According to the statement, the validity of academic ideas should be measured against "intellectual standards of relevant academic and professional disciplines," and the responsibility of judging the merits of competing academic ideas "rests with colleges and universities."[12] This principle protects professorial and institutional academic freedom. While students may disagree with course content or the views of a professor, the institution retains the final say on the merits of academic ideas.

The professional recommendations of AAUP and ACE demonstrate how the higher education community is attempting to balance faculty academic freedom with student rights in the classroom. While neither of these policy statements is controlling, each establishes aspirational benchmarks for the teaching profession.

PROFESSOR ACADEMIC MISCONDUCT

Uncivil conduct of a professor may manifest itself in academic misconduct. This type of misconduct usually occurs when a professor's research and publications fabricate, falsify, or plagiarize.[13] Fabrication involves the creation of artificial data; falsification is the distortion of existing data; and plagiarism relates to copying another's work without attribution.[14]

Evidence suggests that academic misconduct may be a significant problem for professors who conduct research. Several studies indicate that acts of scientific fraud, such as fabricating or manipulating data, appear to be surprisingly common but are likely underreported. One study sponsored by the Office of Research Integrity, an agency that regulates scientific fraud in federally funded research projects, found that an estimated 2,325 possible incidents of illegal research misconduct occurred each year. Many of these incidents occur at colleges and universities that receive federal money to conduct research. However, according to the study, only 58 percent of these occurrences are reported to institutional officials, and an average of only twenty-four investigations are reported annually to the Office of Research Integrity by colleges and universities.[15]

Over the years there have been a number of high-profile cases involving professors who have engaged in academic misconduct. Marc Hauser, a Harvard University psychology professor, was found responsible for eight counts of scientific misconduct in his research on the evolutionary foundations of morality in nonhuman primates. Hauser resigned from his position effective August 1, 2011.[16] In another, Edward Wegman, a George Mason University statistician, drafted an influential 2006 report to Congress criticizing global warming research.[17] Unfortunately, more than one-third of Wegman's ninety-one-page report was plagiarized from other sources, including Wikipedia.[18] In yet another example, Eric T. Poehlman, a former obesity researcher at the University of Vermont, admitted to falsifying and fabricating research data under a $3 million government research grant in 2005.[19]

Claims of academic misconduct are not just limited to scientific research. Joseph J. Ellis, a history professor at Mount Holyoke, fabricated his involvement in the Viet Nam War to students and the media.[20] Ward Churchill, former professor at the University of Colorado, was fired for plagiarizing another professor's essay in a book that Churchill helped edit,[21] and other researchers, professors, and administrators have been cited for sloppy citation at best and academic misconduct at worst on campuses throughout the United States. Although these examples represent a small minority of professors, they reveal a careless disregard for the profession.

In some cases professor academic misconduct occurs in the course of supervising graduate students. According to one ethics survey published by the American Physical Society, 39 percent of graduate students who responded indicated that they had observed or had personal knowledge of ethical violations of a supervising professor. Some participants in the

American Physical Society survey reported being "pressured to overlook data that did not conform to expectations."[22] If this type of unethical behavior persists, the message being sent to students—our future professors and researchers—is that truth is not paramount.

The data suggests that fraud may be the result of intense competition and demands for funding to support scientific research as well as lax self-enforcement by institutions. Academic misconduct by faculty contradicts the truth-seeking attributes of scholarship and professional ethics and undermines academic integrity.

THE CIVIL PROFESSOR

Although professors must grapple with significant civility problems, all is not lost. Overwhelmingly, professors do amazing work for students, their institutions, and society at large. They are dedicated to their discipline and the pursuit of knowledge, and they inspire students to inquire and look for new ways to help students grow intellectually.

Many professors link student learning with community engagement. This blended form of student learning and community involvement is commonly referred to as *service learning*. For example, in the aftermath of Hurricane Katrina, the faculty at Tulane University made service learning a bigger emphasis in its academic curriculum across all academic departments. Ana M. Lopez, the associate professor of communication and associate provost for faculty affairs, told the *Chronicle of Higher Education,* "We felt early that Tulane had a responsibility not only to reopen, but also to help rebuild the city."[23]

The notion of community service has taken on global proportions for some institutions and faculty members. A number of professors at elite colleges and universities are offering free online courses that draw hundreds of thousands of students all over the world. These massive open online courses, or MOOCs, provide cutting-edge college-level instruction to any student with an Internet connection. In 2011, Stanford offered a class on artificial intelligence that enrolled 160,000 students. In 2012,

MIT offered a free online course on circuits and electronics that enrolled more than 120,000 students. Students who successfully complete these courses—typically a small portion of those who enroll—receive certificates of completion. Some experts predict that if credits are earned in these types of classes, they could eventually be transferable to other institutions.

Professors are often excellent role models for demonstrating civility. For example, in 2010, approximately sixty faculty members from the University of California, Irvine published a public statement calling for more civility on campus. At that time, numerous offensive anti-Semitic activities had occurred on campus. Much of the uncivil conduct involved inflammatory rhetoric between Muslim and Jewish student groups on campus. The faculty statement encouraged "open dialogue among all members of the UCI community" but cautioned students against engaging in "hate-promoting actions" that run counter to peaceful coexistence.[24] Whether the statement actually altered student conduct is unknown, but the professors' public call for civility reminded the campus of its community responsibility to maintain a peaceful environment.

Good professors—regardless of their rank—inspire students to learn. They possess the power to change the lives of their students and in turn impact the lives of others through their students. They are not dismissive or hostile but are patient and genuine. They extend mutual respect toward their students and colleagues and engage the community.

Faculty behavior is an essential aspect of promoting civility on campus. The attitudes of professors toward students may have profound implications for learning and civility. Academic leaders should strive to foster alignment of faculty conduct with professional norms and institutional policy and mission.

TOOLS AND EXERCISES

Civil or Uncivil?

Sometimes there is a fine line between civil and uncivil behavior. Many faculty members and adjuncts are noted authorities in their areas of research and have been hired specifically because of their expertise. Some teach courses designed around their professional background or previous study. It seems almost impossible for professors to remain unbiased in their viewpoints, but they are asked to entertain their students' ideas and criticism respectfully and grade based on content and comprehension, not opinion. Some take a genuine interest in their students and actively foster discussion. How often do you think the line between professional knowledge and opinion is blurred? For each of the following scenarios, you decide if the professor crossed the line and explain why or why not.

1. Your political science professor is discussing a unit on risk aversion in international affairs. She states that Saddam Hussein's behaviors and actions represented those of an irrational leader, willing to risk taking on a much greater military force, the United States. She suggests after some class discussion that there might be something associated with Middle Eastern leaders that makes them more likely to engage in risky behavior. *Civil or Uncivil?*

2. You are taking an upper-level English literature course, and its small number of students are on friendly and familiar terms with each other and the professor. You meet once a week to discuss readings. After class one day, your classmate mentions that he got quite a bit out of this week's discussion, especially after having dinner a few days ago at the professor's house where they discussed the material at length. *Civil or Uncivil?*

3. You are at your Biology 101 professor's office to discuss some concepts with which you are having difficulty. He shares his office with another faculty member, and you notice that the room is cramped and messy with boxes and papers covering

his office mate's area. After apologizing for the condition of the room, he remarks, "Can you believe this person got tenure?" *Civil or Uncivil?*

Engaging Civility

Do you believe that professors and institutions have a responsibility to the larger community in which they exist? As shown in the example of Tulane University after Hurricane Katrina, community outreach helped to foster a climate of service and civility in students by encouraging engagement and action while combining it with course work. What are some ways, beyond internships, in which your classes could be applied in your larger community while gaining course credit?

You know, you don't have to be the loser kid in high school to be bullied. Bullying and being picked on comes in so many different forms.

— **Lady Gaga**

CHAPTER 6

Bullying on Campus and in the Workplace

The subject of bullying conjures up images of insensitive childhood pranks occurring on the school playground. Yet bullying is no longer limited to just teasing, stealing someone's lunch money, or giving a wedgie to someone in the restroom. It has become a significant problem in high schools, colleges, and the workplace.

At the collegiate level, bullying has traditionally manifested itself in student hazing, harassment, or discrimination, although the new trend is cyberbullying. Cyberbullies leverage technology to harass their peers persistently through text messages, blogs, social networks, and other forms of electronic communication.

In the workplace, bullies may attempt to spread malicious rumors, undercut coworkers, or constantly degrade peers and subordinates. This toxic conduct is antithetical to a productive workplace and can trigger unexpected consequences. Experts estimate that employers lose billions of dollars every year as a direct result of bullying in the workplace.[1] Bullied employees are more likely to miss work, experience decreased productivity, and ultimately leave their jobs.[2] Replacing even one employee as a result of bullying can cost an employer thousands of dollars in turnover-related costs.[3]

College campuses must deal with bullying among students and also among employees. Bullying is disruptive, diversionary, and generates avoidable conflict. Bullies can completely suck the life out of a vibrant and productive environment. This chapter assesses ways to address bullying and promote mutual respect on campus and in the workplace.

THE CYBERBULLIES AND THE BYSTANDER: SONAM

Stacy Reynolds annoyed just about everyone in her environmental science course. She had a knack for asking absurd and off-point questions that left everyone in the class wondering, *What is she thinking?* The professor, Cindy Porter, actively encouraged questions and discussion during her lectures. When Stacy would start down one of her off-topic bunny trails, Professor Porter did her best to extrapolate something of value from Stacy's "out there" comments; however, most times there was no redemption.

Stacy seemed to be fixated on alternate forms of energy. She constantly interjected this topic into class discussions. For example, in almost every class she spoke of research to use human and animal feces as an alternate form of energy. It was kind of funny and mildly intriguing the first time Stacy made the comment; however, her questions and comments always seemed to go back to creating methane from feces and its promise of being "the fuel of the future."

Over time, whenever Stacy spoke up in class, her classmates moaned audibly. Some students looked at her with disgust while others just wagged their heads in disbelief. Stacy was oblivious to her classmates' disdain. It was clear that Professor Porter did not know how to deal with Stacy's frequent diversions and enthusiasm for discussing energy alternatives.

Sonam was also in Professor Porter's environmental science class. While Sonam found Stacy irritating, Sonam suspected Stacy might have some type of mental disability. Sonam had a cousin with autism whose behavior was strikingly similar to Stacy's. Sonam's cousin Aakar had a similar fixation on elephants. He knew all about elephants—their scientific names, sizes, and unique features. He could talk at length about the differences between African and Asian elephants. When Aakar started talking about elephants, the unsuspecting person might be in for a long lecture.

Sonam did not mind Stacy's classroom diversions. She used the derailed class time to check out what was happening on her social networks. She simply switched from taking notes on her laptop to perusing Facebook, Twitter, and Instagram. On one such occasion, she received a Facebook friend request from "Spacy Methane Reynolds." She nearly laughed out loud in class when she saw the profile picture. It was a picture of a woman sitting on a toilet with Stacy's head superimposed and flying in outer space with what appeared to be rockets on the bottom of the toilet. The picture had a caption that read, "Natural gas that comes out your a**!"

Sonam immediately accepted the friend request. Her new "friend" was actually a fictitious profile that was created by someone in the class to make fun of Stacy. It already had twenty-seven friends, mostly other students from the environmental science class. Whenever Stacy started on one of her tangents, the Spacy Methane Reynolds Facebook page lit up with mean-spirited comments from her classmates. Some comments were more offensive than others. Most contained potty humor. One silly comment read, "Got Feces?" Another simply stated, "Sh*t Happens." Another asked, "Spacy, do you want my Lincoln logs?"

At first, Sonam thought the Facebook page was amusing. It provided a covert way for the disgruntled students to hurl real-time insults when the class was hijacked by Stacy. Whenever someone posted a "good" comment, snickers and laughter could be heard throughout the room. Everyone was in on the joke accept Stacy and Professor Porter.

Over time, Sonam started to have second thoughts. The comments became more offensive and disturbing. One student said, "Conserve more energy by shutting the hell up!" Another posted, "Why don't you just eat sh*t and die!" Other students in the class "liked" these comments and posted even more vile things on the fictitious page.

Sonam knew the Facebook page was intended as a joke, but she was truly bothered by the hurtful and inflammatory comments some of the students were making. Sonom thought, *What if Stacy finds this page? What if Stacy really has some type of mental disability? Maybe she cannot control her disruptive behavior.* Gradually, Sonam began to feel empathy for Stacy.

Sonam knew that if Stacy found out that other students were saying things such as "Why don't you die?" she would be devastated. She contemplated speaking up on the page or maybe saying something in Stacy's defense. She also considered talking with Stacy directly and perhaps politely telling her to scale it back in class. However, she knew that she risked being subjected to similar hostility if she confronted the students who made the hurtful comments on the page. After all, it was just a joke. It was not her job to look after Stacy. Sonam reasoned, *I don't have a dog in this fight.*

Everyone was pleasantly surprised when Stacy did not show up Tuesday morning for environmental science. She had perfect attendance up to that point. Professor Porter looked unusually somber and addressed the class, saying, "Okay, everyone, let's get started." The students began to take their seats and quiet down in preparation for the lecture.

Professor Porter continued, "I have some really sad news. I have just been informed that Stacy Reynolds has committed suicide."

Shock engulfed the room as the word *suicide* hit everyone like a slap in the face. The room fell eerily quiet. Sonam's heart sank into her stomach, and she began to feel physically sick. No one would ever know what caused Stacy to take her life, but Sonam wondered if Stacy found the Facebook page. She wondered what would have happened if she had said something to Stacy or intervened. She fought back tears as she excused herself from the classroom.

UNDERSTANDING THE BULLYING DYNAMIC

Bullying involves the intentional systematic pattern of intimidation and harassment by one person designed to humiliate, frighten, or isolate another.[4] Bullies use their power or influence to intimidate those who are weaker. Regardless of whether bullies are on the playground, the lacrosse team, or the corner office, bullies tend to use the same tactics to harass and annoy. These tactics can be physical (pushing, shoving, or stealing), verbal (spreading rumors, teasing, or taunting), or emotional (shunning, humiliating, or excluding).[5] In most cases bullies act unprovoked and tend to prey on victims who are vulnerable.

In any bullying situation, there are a triad of characters—bullies, targets, and bystanders.[6] The relationship among the three characters is somewhat interdependent.

Bullies

Bullies are the antagonists. The bully's goal is to control and intimidate the target by taking advantage of his or her weakness. These weaknesses may include the target's physical appearance, intellectual abilities, disabilities, or any other attributes that make the target different from others.[7] Many times the bully uses an embarrassing event involving the target. In the opening vignette, Stacy's socially awkward behavior caused her to be a target of harassment. The bully who ultimately set up the fictitious Facebook page created an online venue that allowed others to continually post embarrassing and harassing pictures and comments about Stacy.

A number of complex variables identified by researchers may contribute to a bully's actions. Many bullies have been subjected to bullying, perhaps by a parent or older sibling.[8] Evidence also suggests that bullies may suffer from certain mental health disorders, such as attention deficit disorder or conduct disorders.[9] While many have posited that bullies harass others because they lack sufficient self-esteem, some evidence suggests otherwise. For example, a study conducted by the University of Virginia of nearly four hundred middle school students found that bullies were overwhelmingly considered to be the more popular students in school.[10]

Certain cultural factors may also contribute to bullying. Aggressive in-your-face behavior is often celebrated in our highly competitive culture.[11] The athlete who taunts an opponent on the field, the manager who manipulates a subordinate in the workplace, and the tough-talking politician who uses below-the-belt rhetoric to put down an opponent are often perceived to be winners.

In the workplace the vast majority of bullies hold positions of authority or power within the organization. They tend to be managers, supervisors, and executives. One study found that 70 percent of bullies in the workplace outrank their targets.[12] The power differential that bullies exert over targets makes them untouchable in many organizations.

Targets

Targets are the victims of bullying. Unlike bullies, targets tend to be on the opposite end of the power differential. According to Christine MacDonald, professor of educational and school psychology at Indiana State University, people who are different in some way seem to be singled out by bullies.[13] There are three types of targets who tend to be more susceptible to bullying: (1) targets who are socially exposed; (2) targets who are socially incompetent; and (3) targets who do not fit the group's norm.[14]

Targets who are socially exposed are often members of a minority group. A homosexual student who attends a conservative religious university and a female who works in a department dominated by male employees are examples of socially exposed targets.

Socially incompetent targets tend to be unassertive, possess low self-esteem, and experience high anxiety. These targets may have been subjected to bullying earlier in life. When socially incompetent targets are pushed, they rarely push back. Accordingly, they are easy prey for bullies.

Targets who do not fit group norms are generally confident overachievers, who possess skills that the bullies do not have.[15] The bully, feeling threatened or annoyed by the target, exposes the target to harassment as a way to improve his or her own social standing.

Regardless of age, the effects of bullying on targets can be profoundly destructive. Targets may suffer loss of concentration, anxiety, insomnia, and even post-traumatic stress disorder.[16] These conditions may impact the target's academic and work performance, as well as mental health. Victims may also suffer depression, decreased self-worth, hopelessness, and loneliness, which are often precursors to suicidal ideations.[17] Over the last several years there has been a string of high-profile bullying-related suicides, which some researchers have termed *bullycide*.[18]

Stacy was clearly a target of bullying. Perhaps her suicide was the result of finding the fictitious Facebook page and reading the hateful comments directed toward her. Reading such hurtful comments from peers would be painfully difficult for anyone and could destroy a person's sense of self-worth.

Bystanders

As the name suggests, bystanders are the people who witness the bullying.[19] When bystanders observe bullying, they must make a complicated choice. They can choose to turn a blind eye and avoid getting involved, they can join in the harassment, or they can try to intervene.

Like Sonam, the overwhelming majority of bystanders choose *not* to intervene. Many are afraid that intervening might make them the next targets of harassment. Sometimes bystanders mistakenly assume that the bullying is harmless or done in jest. In these situations, the bystanders may even participate in the harassment, justifying the conduct as a harmless joke.

When a target is harassed by multiple bullies, the conduct is called *mobbing*.[20] The Spacy Methane Reynolds Facebook page was an example of mobbing. Many students in the class participated in making embarrassing and harassing posts on the page. Although the harassment occurred online, the impact of finding such a hateful site filled with mean-spirited comments would most likely be crushing. Harassment by one bully can cause severe emotional harm, but the experience of being mobbed by a number of bullies can be psychologically devastating.

Many bystanders want to help, but they do not know how. Intervening takes courage, especially when the bully is popular, is well liked, or is a boss. Self-preservation often prevents bystanders from intervening. This reaction is certainly understandable. Confronting the bully could put the bystander's social status or even career in jeopardy.

There really is no bright line rule defining how bystanders should respond to a bully. Depending on the situation, direct intervention could be problematic. In the right situation, making a simple statement like, "Okay, that's enough," or taking steps to change the subject could provide temporary relief to the target.

However, direct intervention is not the only option for bystanders. Bystanders can indirectly intervene in ways that may actually be more effective. For example, a bystander can make a big difference by making an effort to acknowledge the target, taking the time to listen, and offering encouragement and emotion support.[21] A target commonly seeks support from a friend, colleague, or coworker.[22] One study concluded that talking with a trusted friend or coworker was one of the most effective methods for dealing with bullying. It was actually more effective than reporting the bully.

STUDENT BULLYING IN HIGHER EDUCATION

Until recently, bullying in the context of higher education has not received much attention from researchers,[23] but new data is emerging.

According to a 2011 study conducted by researchers at Indiana State University, 15 percent of the college students surveyed reported being bullied and 22 percent reported being cyberbullied.[24] The two forms of bullying that are likely to occur on campus are hazing and cyber bullying.

Hazing

Most people desire acceptance. Students are no exception, especially when they are new on campus. However, when acceptance into a group requires some form of initiation that humiliates, degrades, or risks emotional or physical harm, the group has engaged in hazing.[25] Hazing, like bullying, involves an abuse of power, control, and intimidation. However, while bullying can happen to anyone and is used to *exclude* individuals from a group, hazing is limited to individuals who wish to become a member of a group and is used to *include* individuals into a group.[26]

Hazing has been part of higher education since after the Civil War.[27] During this time, military veterans who had reentered college introduced the practice of hazing to college campuses. Hazing involved boot-camp-style conditioning methods where the dominant members of a group subjected the subordinate members to physical and psychological abuse. Hazing first gained popularity among fraternities and sororities. The practice was steeped in secrecy and tradition and was used to build trust and camaraderie. Today hazing continues to be an issue in higher education and occurs in other student groups, such as athletic teams, marching bands, professional schools, church groups, and other social and academic clubs. In fact, more than half of the students who belong to campus organizations experienced hazing.[28]

Hazing typically involves coercing alcohol consumption but may also include requiring pledges to endure sleep deprivation, undergo physical and verbal abuse, engage in humiliating sex acts, or participate in strenuous physical activity.[29] Some students might view hazing as harmless pranks, but the practice often results in serious injuries and sometimes death. Since 1970, there has been at least one hazing-related death on a college campus each year.[30]

Over the last three years, there have been several high-profile hazing incidents. The death of Robert Champion, a drum major in Florida A&M's high-profile marching band, broke into the headlines in 2011. According to university officials, Champion was punched repeatedly by a small group of band members on a bus following a football game. He suffered blunt trauma blows to his body and died from shock caused by severe bleeding. Several band members were charged with third-degree felony hazing, and two students were charged with manslaughter, which carries a penalty of up to fifteen years in prison.[31] Since the charges were filed, seven of the band members have accepted pleas that included probation and community service-related sentences.[32] At the time of this writing, another band member has pleaded, but hasn't been sentenced, and the rest are still awaiting trial.[33]

That same year the Pi Kappa Alpha fraternity chapter at the University of Tennessee introduced the world to "butt chugging"—a process by which alcohol is consumed anally.[34] The butt chugging came to light after a twenty-year-old student at the University of Tennessee was taken to the emergency room after passing out with a blood alcohol level of nearly .45, more than five times the legal limit. The hospital staff became concerned when they found that the student also had rectal injuries.[35] According to a police incident report, another student had made a statement that the injured student and other members of the fraternity were butt chugging wine. Although the injured student denied the claim, a number of the students involved with the incident were charged with underage drinking, and the fraternity was temporarily disbanded.[36]

In 2012, Cornell University banned its Tau Epsilon Phi fraternity when two pledges were hospitalized following a sexually humiliating hazing incident. Pledges were told to strip down to their underwear and then existing members violently ripped them off. Alcohol was involved in this incident.

In 2013, engineering students at Ryerson University, in Toronto, Canada, were criticized for an annual ritual that was reminiscent of hazing.[37] Students wanting to be considered for leadership positions in the student engineering society were urged to army crawl through snow and slush outside a campus building while wearing only their underwear or swimsuits. A YouTube video of the ritual went viral and showed older engineering students wearing blue coveralls squirting participants with water guns and hitting participants with snowballs.[38] The engineering students responsible for the ritual did not characterize the event as hazing and pointed out that students are not required to strip and leadership opportunities are still available for students who do not participate.[39]

Hazing is illegal in most states, and in some states it is considered a felony. Despite the fact that hazing could be a criminal offense, the practice still occurs. Students affected by hazing rarely report the incidents, perhaps because nine out of ten students who have experienced hazing do not consider themselves to have been hazed.[40]

The notion that acceptance into a group would be based on enduring violent physical attacks, putting up with demeaning sexual assaults by peers, and ingesting alcohol rectally is disturbing. Nevertheless, students seeking acceptance into certain groups often voluntarily subject themselves to hazing, while existing members readily participate in acts that put new members in danger. It could be that students do not fully appreciate the gravity of hazing. Many see hazing as harmless pranks. Others view hazing as a rite of passage or a time-honored tradition that must be continued. However, in most states students who haze can be sent to jail.

When hazing is assessed in the context of civility, it is helpful to think about whether the practice promotes mutual respect and dignity. Is the community strengthened when existing members use a power differential to coerce others to engage in dangerous activities against their will? Probably not. Furthermore, there may be intense social pressure not to report hazing incidents. No one likes a snitch. However, when the health and safety of another are in jeopardy, reporting could save a life.

Campus Cyberbullies

Cyberbullying made national headlines in 2010 when Tyler Clementi, a freshman at Rutgers University, committed suicide just three days after learning that his roommate had used a webcam to spy on him while he was kissing another man in his room. While no one will really know whether the humiliation of the webcam spying caused Clementi to commit suicide, it was likely a significant contributing factor.

Cyberbullying is perpetrated when a bully leverages technology and electronic communication, such as e-mails, texts, instant messages, and social media, to harass a target. When the bullying occurs in cyberspace, the harassment knows no boundaries. It can occur virtually anywhere and at any time. For example, the bully can easily bombard a target with harassing e-mails and text messages, spread rumors about the target on social media, or post humiliating private information about the target on message boards, blogs, and even YouTube. According to the Pew Internet and American Life Project, one in three teens has experienced online harassment.[41]

The psychological impact of cyberbullying can be overwhelming. Students who were subjected to cyberbullying may experience depression, anxiety, and paranoia.[42] Once a bully has access to damaging information regarding the target—whether true or false—widespread dissemination can be accomplished effortlessly. Using technology, the bully is able to subject a target to humiliation and ridicule online way beyond the confines of the campus. In cyberspace, this electronic information has the capacity to go viral and literally spread around the world.

For example, the recent trend among students of sharing sexually suggestive pictures or video via mobile phones, or sexting, creates new opportunities for cyberbullies. Geovany Alarcon, a San Jose State University student, was sentenced to four years in prison in a case involving sexting.[43] In this case Alarcon, a twenty-year-old male, met a seventeen-year-old girl from Colorado on MySpace. Alarcon requested that she send him sexually explicit images and videos of herself. The girl complied with the request.

The student then requested that she molest a younger girl and send a video of the act. Alarcon warned that if the female student did not comply, he would distribute her sexually explicit pictures and videos to her friends and family, whom he knew because the two were friends on MySpace. The girl eventually told her mother what was going on, and law enforcement intervened. Alarcon was arrested and pleaded guilty to sexual exploitation of a minor.[44]

With just the click of a mouse it is very easy for information to go viral with embarrassing and unexpected consequences. In one example, a 2010 Duke University graduate e-mailed a few friends a spoof thesis rating her sexual experiences with several Duke athletes.[45] The email included a PowerPoint presentation, complete with commentary and pictures. Within months the e-mail, with the attached PowerPoint, went viral and created a media frenzy.

Unlike traditional bullying, many forms of cyberbullying have the potential to remain in the digital domain indefinitely. Through the Internet, the bully can potentially expose the victim to international embarrassment, which can have damaging effects on the victim's personal, social, and professional lives.

WORKPLACE BULLYING

In 2010, Kevin Morrissey's suicide made headlines when his family and friends attributed his death to bullying in the workplace.[46] Morrissey was the managing editor of the *Virginia Quarterly Review*, a literary journal published by the University of Virginia. Morrissey's supervisor, Ted Genoways, was accused by several members of his small staff as being a bully.[47]

Over a period of two years, Morrissey repeatedly complained about Genoways's abusive supervisory behavior to university officials. He even used a faculty and employee assistance program to intervene in the conflict. However, these efforts resulted in no corrective actions. The human resources manager advised Morrissey to file a formal complaint against his supervisor to no avail.[48] Morrissey committed suicide.

The close proximity between Morrissey's complaints and suicide caused the university to conduct an investigation of Genoways's conduct. The investigation found evidence of Genoways's lack of courtesy and respect and that he had used "questionable management skills."[49] Other people filed a number of informal complaints about Genoways's erratic behavior. Yet the university concluded that the complaints never rose to a level of a serious and ongoing concern; in other words, Genoways was not a bully. Shortly after Morrissey's suicide, almost all of Genoways's staff left.[50]

Morrissey's estate filed a lawsuit against the University of Virginia, Genoways, and several university officials, including the former president, seeking more than $10 million in damages. The lawsuit alleged that university officials were negligent in failing to address Morrissey's claims of abuse, which allegedly drove him to commit suicide.[51]

Morrissey's suicide vividly illustrates how incivility in the workplace can escalate into violence, negatively affect other employees, and impact an entire institution. While Morrissey clearly made multiple attempts to follow the university's policies to address the offending conduct, his efforts did not result in meaningful intervention. Even though other complaints were filed against Genoways, the university concluded his conduct was not serious enough to merit intervention.

The challenge for employers is how to address bullying among its employees. It is difficult to fault the University of Virginia for failing to take more substantive measures when the alleged harassment involved subjective concepts of courtesy and respect. Currently, there are no laws that prohibit managers, coworkers, or colleagues from bullying each other unless the conduct involves some form of assault, battery, or discrimination based on race, gender, disability, or other federally protected class. When an employee is the target of bullying that is nonphysical or does not involve discrimination, there may be few options available to prevent the harassment.

EFFECTS OF BULLYING

Bullying in the workplace often goes unnoticed. Bullies may be unaware their conduct is offensive. Many workplaces have an ingrained culture of incivility, so bullying may be the norm. Often targets are hesitant to report the offending conduct because they do not wish to be seen as complainers out of fear of retribution. Moreover, even if victims were to report, there is often no process to address the harassment adequately. Nevertheless, taking proactive steps to address bullying is critical for employers because failing to address bullying can create a highly ineffective and dysfunctional workplace as shown in the example at the University of Virginia.

One of the main reasons that employers should take bullying seriously is the greatly diminished employee productivity caused by the conduct. Robert Sutton, management professor at Stanford University, estimates that productivity declines as much as 40 percent in workplaces dominated by bullies.[52] Productivity is impaired because targets tend to take more sick leaves and have higher rates of absenteeism.

Employers should also address bullying because of the severe psychological harm it causes targets. Targets of bullying may suffer from clinical depression, panic attacks, and even post-traumatic stress disorder. In fact, the American Psychological Association (APA) has found that the psychological impact of dealing with workplace bullying may be more harmful than sexual harassment.[53] These severe psychological impairments may affect the target's ability to focus and concentrate at work, create workers' compensation claims for stress, and result in costly litigation expenses.

Another important reason employers should focus on bullying is that the persistent conduct may drive away good employees. According to the U.S. Hostile Workplace Survey, 38 percent of bullied employees left voluntarily.[54] Bullying may also drive coworkers who are bystanders out the door.[55]

The effect of these findings comes into sharper focus when one considers the significant financial costs associated with replacing employees, especially those who are highly trained and experienced. According to a 2011 AARP study, turnover-related costs, which often include recruitment, training, severance pay, and lost productivity, can be 50 percent or more of the exiting employee's annual salary.[56] Employers should seriously consider the potential financial impact of replacing highly skilled works as a result of incivility. Losing just one employee to bullying could cost the institution thousands of dollars.

The bottom line for employers is that bullying may have a real financial impact. Whether the impact is lost productivity, turnover-related costs, or defense of a lawsuit from a harassed employee, employers can expend an enormous amount of time, energy, and resources because of issues that could have been averted. Developing an engaged, productive, and civil workplace creates an environment that promotes positive morale and encourages meaningful investment into the organization by everyone.

PROMOTING CIVILITY ON CAMPUS AND IN THE WORKPLACE

Colleges and universities are usually very open and accepting communities for students and employees. Most offer a diverse array of student activities, clubs, and organizations. Higher education institutions often promote programs to encourage student engagement and facilitate student integration into the campus community. There is typically a place for everyone to fit in. Nevertheless, bullying continues to be a growing issue for many campuses.

Colleges and universities can play an important role in promoting civility on campus. Civility is advanced when there is an institutional emphasis on community values—values such as respecting diverse people and ideas, serving the community, and maintaining an open and accepting learning environment. These values must be reinforced in the classroom, in student housing, and in academic departments. If these values can be instilled in students, students will likely carry these values into their professional careers after graduation.

Bullying is often a topic covered in first-year student seminars and courses. Academic departments often invite speakers and consultants to provide guidance on dealing with bullying among administrators, faculty, and staff. Many schools conduct special symposia or panel discussions on the issue of bullying that are open to the campus and the community. While these events are not going to eliminate bullying on campus, they create a helpful dialogue and underscore the institution's commitment to civil discourse and engagement. Students and faculty often deeply misunderstand what type of conduct might constitute bullying and its detrimental effects on the target, the bystanders, and the entire community.

Outside of higher education, many employers are taking proactive steps to promote a more respectful working environment and a culture of civility. These employers have discovered many tangible and financial benefits from having a bully-free workplace.

The Internet giant Google provides numerous innovative perks for its employees, some of which contribute to a more civil work environment. They include subsidized massages, a wellness center, and a seven-acre sports complex comprised of everything from basketball courts to a roller hockey rink.[57] Google employees, called "Googlers," also enjoy a work environment that celebrates cultural diversity.[58] The company offers prayer rooms, mothers' rooms, day care, domestic partnership programs, and robust accommodations for people who are disabled.[59]

The Boston Consulting Group takes employee work-life balance seriously. This elite consulting firm issues what it calls a "red zone report" to flag when individuals are working too much. The firm is also civically minded. It encourages employees to volunteer at nonprofit organizations.[60]

FedEx is another company that encourages its employees to volunteer in their communities. The annual FedEx Cares Week gives FedEx team members across the globe "the opportunity to make a difference in their own communities." During the September 2012 FedEx Cares Week, more than 4,000 FedEx employees volunteered in over 186 local projects in 67 countries. FedEx has also demonstrated a commitment to maintaining its workforce. Recently when the company encountered economic challenges, it eliminated "several thousand positions," not with mass across-the-board layoffs but with voluntary buyouts.[61]

Wegmans Food Markets, a northeastern grocery chain, allows employees to "reward one another with gift cards for good services." Interestingly, this grocer's employee turnover rate is only 3.6 percent.[62]

Coyote Logistics, a Chicago-based company specializing in ground transportation, promotes workplace cohesion by focusing on new hires who would "be a cultural fit." The company has a policy of "hiring smart people out of college, regardless of their major" and tends to hire friends of employees.[63]

These businesses are just a small sample of the many that are striving to promote civility in the workplace. They reward good service, encourage community engagement, and emphasize an appropriate balance between work and life. These employers recognize the diversity of their employees and understand that this diversity brings unique perspectives that are crucial to understanding an increasingly global marketplace. They invest in their employees, and their employees return the investment with commitment, productivity, and innovation.

A civil campus and workplace are not places where everyone always agrees and are free of contention, but they are places where differences are vetted respectfully, without malicious personal attacks, threats, or verbal harassment.

TOOLS AND EXERCISES

Bullying Policy on Campus

Bullying awareness has increased exponentially in recent years. Yet many institutions of higher education lack specific policies regarding bullying, effectively leaving targets of bullying to handle a complex situation alone. Most agree that colleges and universities have a responsibility to provide a safe and supportive learning environment, but sometimes administrators may be reluctant to intervene, preferring to regard bullying as more of a "kids being kids" phenomenon. How does your college approach bullying? Imagine you are speaking with the dean of students at your college and asking the following questions. Investigate on your school Web site or speak with an administrator to find answers.

1. Does this institution have a bullying policy that applies to students and faculty? If not, is this something that is seen as a priority?
2. If one does exist, to whom does a student or instructor report bullying, and who intervenes?
3. What disciplinary action—if any—exists?
4. Does the college have a bullying awareness educational program as part of student orientation or as a requirement? If not, how might one be developed?
5. What are the costs of implementing such a program? What are the costs of not doing so?

The Bystander Challenge

Review the vignette, "The Cyberbullies and the Bystander," at the beginning of chapter 6 featuring Sonam and Stacy, and answer the following questions:

1. Do you think Sonam was involved in the bullying of Stacy even though she might never have posted on the Facebook page? Explain.
2. What if Stacy had never found out about the Facebook page? What are the implications of bullying even if the person is unaware of being a target of ridicule?
3. Do you think the bullying would have ceased if the students knew Stacy had some kind of disability?
4. Did Sonam have a responsibility to report the page to someone at the school?
5. Think about a time when you have witnessed bullying. How did you handle it? What might you have done differently, if anything?
6. Have you been bullied? What would you like others to know about that experience?

Give me your tired, your poor, Your huddled masses,
yearning to breath free, The wretched refuse of your
teeming shore, Send these, the homeless, tempest tost
to me, I lift my lamp beside the golden door.
Inscription on **The Statue of Liberty**

CHAPTER 7

Diversity

D iversity is in the DNA of American culture. From its inception,
the United States has been a nation of immigrants who have come
from all corners of the world. From the eighteen million European
immigrants who migrated to America between 1890 and 1920 to the
estimated more than eleven million undocumented primarily Latino
immigrants who currently live among us, people come to the United
States to seek a better life.[1]

America has been described as a melting pot. This metaphor is used to
illustrate how people of vastly different races, colors, cultures, and beliefs
can be transformed into American citizens with common American values.
Immigrants who come to the United States do not abandon their culture
and heritage; for the most part they and succeeding generations become
part of the diverse multicultural tapestry of American society.

This diversity of people, cultures, and ideas is often the impetus
for innovation. From science and technology to art and entertainment,
America is known for its innovation. Yet Americans have not always

recognized or appreciated the benefits of diversity. Throughout history the people of the United States have grappled with how to coexist peacefully with people of different races, ethnicities, genders, and religious beliefs. Minority groups have had to overcome discriminatory laws, policies, and practices and work to dispel irrational stereotypes and prejudices.

Although the United States has made significant progress toward embracing its diversity, many question the validity of the melting pot concept. Hot button issues such as affirmative action and illegal immigration trigger concerns about the fair allocation of limited resources and opportunities. Americans have become increasingly suspect of Muslims since the 9/11 terrorist attacks in 2001. Recent efforts by Muslims to build community centers and mosques have met with stiff opposition and legal action. The recognition of gay marriage has challenged our society's traditional definition of marriage and has created deep societal schisms. Political parties vie for support based on ideologically divergent worldviews on these and many other issues. The resulting polarization has resulted in political deadlock, preventing the country from dealing with key issues.

In a society that tends to self-segregate, diverse groups of people need to respect differences, be more understanding of other points of view, and attempt to reach meaningful consensus on divisive issues affecting our communities. Colleges and universities can play an important role in helping students develop a better appreciation for diverse people and ideas. Acquiring the skill set to live, learn, and grow in a diverse college community has critical applications both in the marketplace and in the community.

This chapter examines the interplay between diversity and civility on the college campus. Exposure to diverse people, culture, beliefs, and ideas is occurring in an increasingly global society. Such exposure often provides new perspectives and greater appreciation for differences. It may also dispel stereotypes and prejudices. While we are all uniquely different, our differences may not be as profound as are our common bonds as American citizens.

FREE AT LAST: ANTONIO

Antonio Juarez often considered himself a minority within a minority. He was interracial—his father was Puerto Rican, and his mother was of German descent. Antonio jokingly referred to himself as a "Puerto German." To look at Antonio, one would probably not immediately recognize his Latino background. His skin was only marginally darker than most of his friends who were Caucasian. His facial features, light brown hair, and green eyes were more consistent with his European ancestry. He did not have an accent and did not speak Spanish. By all accounts he had a typical middle-class American upbringing. While his name was a constant reminder of his dual heritage, he downplayed his minority status.

Ethnicity was not really an issue for Antonio. He never saw people based on their skin color or nationality. He liked to hang with people who were fun—people who shared his interests, regardless of their ethnicity, religion, or any other factor. The issue of ethnicity came into sharper focus during Antonio's freshman year. His fraternity had thrown a Dirty Mexican party, creating an uproar on campus. While Antonio thought the idea for the party was hilarious and had no intention to hurt anyone, the entire event was based on offensive racial stereotypes. Many minority and international students were deeply offended by the demeaning characterization of Mexicans. If Antonio was honest, he would not have wanted his parents to know that he had participated in the event. After the event, Antonio began to appreciate the unique challenges that minorities faced in higher education and began to notice the underrepresentation of Latinos and other minorities on his campus. It was not a laughing matter.

During his sophomore year Antonio decided to join the Latin American Student Organization (LASO). This group was organized to promote cultural awareness of Spanish-speaking cultures, but it also was a valuable social venue for Latino students on campus. LASO was one of several multicultural student organizations on campus. By the end of the fall semester, Antonio had really connected with the other students in LASO. Although he was only half Puerto Rican and did not speak Spanish, the other students accepted him. He enjoyed meeting other

Latin American students on campus and quickly realized they had a lot in common. He decided to take Spanish as an elective during the spring semester. He was challenged in a new way to embrace his Puerto Rican heritage and learn more about his cultural roots.

In January, LASO decided to join other groups on campus and charter a bus to Washington, D.C., to participate in the Civil Rights Yesterday and Today Conference. The event was scheduled during the weekend of the Martin Luther King Jr. holiday and included a number of forums on civil rights, featuring past and present leaders in the movement. There were also opportunities for participants to volunteer and engage in community service in the Washington, D.C., area. The event culminated in a rally at the Lincoln Memorial where Dr. King delivered his famous "I Have a Dream" speech in 1963.

Antonio decided to take this trip in part because Brittany Garcia was going—someone Antonio hoped to get to know better—and in part because the subject really intrigued him. Inequality among ethnic and racial groups was a complicated issue. Antonio did not subscribe to the view that disparities were based solely on public policy or institution-wide oppression. He believed that individuals must bear some, if not most, of the responsibility for their own advancement. American society had changed dramatically since Dr. King advocated for civil rights in the 1950s and 1960s. Antonio's very existence as a child from an interracial marriage was tangible proof of the changing attitudes toward race in American culture. Antonio thought the election of Barack Obama as president of the United States was another important milestone for race relations and a continuation of Dr. King's dream.

Antonio also considered the differences he noticed in his own family. His dad did not attend college, and most of the people on the Puerto Rican side of his family either worked in manufacturing or were employed in technical or service-related work. Many of his cousins started families early, arguably too early. He was one of the few members of the family who aspired to attend a four-year college. Although his parents were proud of his decision to attend college and were extremely supportive, his extended family remained indifferent.

His family on his mother's side was more affluent, and his mom had a college degree in accounting. Higher education was very important to that family. His grandparents actually set aside money for their grandchildren to attend college. While the amount did not cover everything, it helped to defray the cost significantly. The majority of Antonio's aunts and uncles had college degrees and were employed in professional careers.

Antonio chalked up the differences between his dad's and mom's families as normal. Setting race aside, he observed many different types of family dynamics and divergent family values. Nevertheless, he wondered whether past racial discrimination had set a trajectory that affected his father's family, a trajectory that was only now beginning to change.

Thousands of college students from all over the country participated in the Civil Rights Yesterday and Today Conference. Antonio got the chance to meet Brittany, and they served together painting classrooms in a public school during the day of community service and walked together to the final rally at the Lincoln Memorial on Monday morning.

Thousands of people stood in front of the Lincoln Memorial as a leader from the NAACP read aloud Dr. King's "I Have a Dream" speech. The audience listened in quiet reverence as the speaker read the last line of the speech:

> *When we allow freedom to ring—when we let it ring from every city and every hamlet, from every state and every city, we will be able to speed up that day when all of God's children, black men and white men, Jews and Gentiles, Protestants and Catholics, will be able to join hands and sing in the words of the old Negro spiritual, "Free at last, Free at last, Great God a-mighty, We are free at last."*

As the National Mall erupted in applause, Antonio stopped for a moment and looked around at the kaleidoscope of people who took part in the conference: young and old, black and white, Hispanic and Asian people, and even interracial people. He thought, *Perhaps this is a glimmer of what Dr. King envisioned.*

STRENGTH IN DIVERSITY

In our ever-changing interconnected world, exposure to diverse people is a tremendous benefit. Understanding diverse cultures, customs, and beliefs fosters deeper appreciation and respect for the people in our community. It provides new perspectives for better understanding diverse people and unique approaches to assessing problems and solutions.

The business world often touts diversity as being integral to innovation. When an organization is filled with people who all think alike, no matter how smart the people are, they are likely to miss opportunities. Finding new and better solutions requires thinking differently. Silicon Valley is an excellent example of diversity and innovation. Technology firms in Silicon Valley attract the best and the brightest engineers from all over the world. The end result is that this technology hub has been able to out innovate other technology hot spots with equal brainpower but less diversity.[2]

In the realm of business, diversity allows an organization to tap into many different experiences, perspectives, and skills to generate new ideas, technologies, and insights. Innovative ideas can be incredibly valuable to both the business and society.[3] They can transform institutions, enterprises, and even society as a whole. Consider the impact of Thomas Edison's light bulb, Wilbur and Orville Wright's airplane, or the Apple iPhone.

Diversity is also critical to institutions of higher education. According to a study conducted by Patricia Gurin at the University of Michigan, diverse learning environments help students communicate and work effectively with people of varied backgrounds and cultures. These skills are essential for college graduates in an increasingly complex and interconnected world. Learning in a diverse environment prepares students to thrive in the global marketplace.[4] Diversity also improves classroom discussion, enhancing the experience for all participants. Faculty and students from diverse backgrounds provide unique insights into subject matter based on their cultures, beliefs, and experiences. Exposure to a diverse student body also promotes cross-cultural understanding, an important goal for furthering civility.

Attending an institution of higher education is often the first opportunity for many students from different backgrounds to coexist. On any given college campus, there are students of varying races, nationalities, ages, socioeconomic backgrounds, sexual orientations, religions, and political affiliations. Diverse students are able to live, learn, and socialize on campus in ways that are less likely to happen off campus. These interactions are valuable and essential to giving students a firsthand opportunity to engage and interact with people from diverse groups. However, the convergence of diverse people on campus can also generate conflict.

DIVERSITY CHALLENGES ON CAMPUS

The first colleges established in the United States were essentially homogenous institutions, enrolling men from elite families of European descent. Separate colleges for women followed. African Americans did not have access to higher education—many were still legally slaves. This all began to change in 1837 when Oberlin College became the first to enroll both men and women and one of the first to admit African American students. After Oberlin cracked the gender and racial barriers, institutions of higher education have often found themselves in the center of issues involving social change.

Over the last two centuries, colleges and universities have had to grapple with how to unlock educational opportunities for underrepresented populations, including individuals of different races, national origins, religions, genders, disabilities, and sexual orientations. The push behind these struggles and eventual changes was a desire to provide equal access to higher education and to create college campuses that were as diverse as the citizens of America. When institutions revised their policies to become more inclusive or respond to societal changes, they often met opposition.

When some were slow to respond, they sometimes were required by legal and legislative action to change.

In 1964, Congress passed Title VI of the Civil Rights Act. This law prohibited higher education institutions from discriminating against students based on race, color, or national origin. This law eventually led to affirmative action programs among colleges and universities to recruit minority students. These programs were criticized as being a reverse form of discrimination. Some programs granted minority students admission and scholarships based on race.

The U.S. Supreme Court has struck down affirmative action programs that were based on quotas or established separate admissions policies for minority students.[5] While race may be a factor in the admissions process, it cannot be the *only* factor. According to the U.S. Supreme Court, race may be considered a positive factor in an admissions decision if it is "narrowly tailored" to foster educational diversity.[6] However, diversity must not be limited to just race and ethnicity. Colleges and universities must consider other characteristics that would contribute to a more diverse student body.[7] The Supreme Court recently reaffirmed its earlier decisions that race remains a legitimate factor to consider in achieving diversity on campus.[8] However, the Court noted that colleges and universities have the ultimate burden of demonstrating that available workable race-neutral alternatives do not suffice before turning to racial classifications.[9]

Despite federal law and institutional policies that prohibit discrimination based on race, color, or national origin, minority students are still occasionally subject to harassment and discrimination. As recently as March 2013, Oberlin College had to cancel classes after a string of racially charged hate-related incidents occurred on campus.[10] First, someone defaced a number of Black History Month posters displayed on campus with the word *Nigger*.[11] Next, students found a "Whites Only" sign above a water fountain and a swastika drawn on a science center window. Classes were canceled when a person wearing a hooded robe resembling that of the Ku Klux Klan was seen near an African heritage building. These incidents triggered an FBI investigation.

On November 7, 2012, more than four hundred Ole Miss students reacted to the reelection of President Barack Obama by gathering at the student union to protest the results. Students chanted political slogans and shouted racial epithets. The protest was dispersed by campus police, and no one was injured.[12]

In 2010, University of Tennessee students made headlines when they threw bananas at more than two hundred visiting African American students, their parents, and guidance counselors.[13]

These are just a few examples of racial tensions that continue to exist on college campuses. Although America's population is increasingly racially and ethnically diverse, most college campuses do not reflect this diversity. According to latest figures from the U.S. Census Bureau, 76 percent of all college students are white.[14]

When diverse groups arrive on campus, it can be challenging to encourage integration among students. Students tend to gravitate toward others with similar backgrounds. Because of stereotypes and prejudices, both majority and minority students may feel apprehensive about associating with students from other groups. Students in minority groups may feel isolated from the larger campus community.

DIVERSITY IN COMMUNITIES

According to the 2010 census, approximately one in three Americans is a minority. While the majority of the population is white, there has been a surge in minority populations, especially among the Hispanic and Asian populations. In fact, demographers estimate that the United States is on a trajectory toward reaching a "majority-minority" population in the next thirty years.[15] A majority-minority population is one in which all races and ethnicities belong to minority groups that make up a complex whole; in other words, no racial or ethnic group has a majority.

In addition to racial and ethnic diversity, the United States is religiously diverse. There is no state or official religion, and Americans are free to worship as they please. Historically, a majority of Americans have been affiliated with Protestant faiths. Yet that is changing. The Pew Forum on Religion and Public Life estimates that the United States is on the verge of becoming a country in which Protestants are in the minority.[16]

The face of America is rapidly changing and to some extent has created an identity crisis in our democratic society. The historically white male, Protestant majority now must seriously consider minorities, women, and people of different faiths and beliefs. Moreover, diversity is not evenly distributed throughout the country. The greatest diversity tends to be in the largest population centers. For example, California and Texas together have nearly one-third of all the nation's minorities. In contrast, the Midwest, some northeastern states, and rural areas of the country tend to be less racially diverse.

Although America is statistically diverse, many people have limited exposure to this diversity. Even people who live in diverse communities may not have meaningful exposure to diversity. Diverse groups tend to self-segregate based on similar characteristics, such as race, ethnicity, religion, and political affiliation. These homogenous groups can become so insulated that they are completely oblivious to other people in the community. This isolation fosters misunderstandings and stereotypes about others, which students bring with them when they enter college.

Stereotypes

A *stereotype* is a generalized assumption that all members of a certain group possess the same qualities and characteristics.[17] Stereotypes are difficult to avoid, especially when an individual has had little or no exposure to people in the stereotyped group. For example, some common stereotypes are that all gay men are flamboyant and feminine, all blacks are superior athletes, and people who speak with a southern accent are less intelligent. These stereotypes overlook the individuality of a person and presume that everyone of a certain group has the same characteristics, values, opinions, or behaviors. The end result is overgeneralization, which can lead to unmerited bias and even prejudice and discrimination.

Stereotypes are very complex and involve numerous psychological and environmental factors. Some social psychologists believe that stereotypes are an involuntary response to our natural tendency to categorize.[18] People tend to group others based on easily identifiable categories, such as age, race, gender, religion, or political affiliation.[19] Over time people learn to associate certain characteristics with certain groups.[20] Stereotypes may also be developed when the members of one group have little contact with other outside groups.[21] This lack of integration between diverse groups may make it easier for stereotypes to be formed. Many believe that the media reinforces stereotypes.[22] Movies, television, and advertising frequently incorporate stereotypes about age, race, gender, and religion.

Overcoming stereotypes and prejudices is essential to achieving an inclusive and diverse community, but the harmonious integration of diverse groups can prove to be extremely challenging. Differences between groups can create schisms that may further perpetuate stereotypes and lead to prejudice and discrimination. While most people do not consider themselves to be prejudiced, people may continue to associate negative stereotypes with certain groups. Lurking below the surface, the stereotypes are often exposed unintentionally.

Prejudice

Prejudice is when a person forms inflexible and irrational attitudes and opinions regarding members of a particular group. Prejudice is not based on experience; instead it is a prejudgment originating outside actual experience. Research has shown that prejudice is fundamentally related to low self-esteem. By espousing irrational attitudes and opinions regarding certain groups, prejudiced people are able to enhance their feelings of self-worth and importance.

Since the enactment of the Civil Rights Act, prejudice is no longer blatant. Although job announcements no longer state "Whites Only" or "Blacks Need Not Apply," prejudice exists. It has just gone underground. Modern prejudice tends to occur implicitly and is characterized by an automatic and unconscious expression.[23] Prejudices are often passed on from parents to children. These prejudices may be further reinforced by depictions in television, movies, and advertising.

People may intend to be fair-minded, but subconsciously they may jump to conclusions that activate stereotypes and ignore contradictory information.[24] For example, an employer may unthinkingly practice sexism by not considering females for certain positions traditionally held by men.[25] Others may have strong prejudices against certain people but choose not to act on them. A business owner may think homosexuals are "an abomination" or immigrants should "go home," but he or she would not consciously discriminate against them. While people might not be aware of their prejudices or would never acknowledge their prejudices publicly, they may inadvertently treat individuals carelessly.

Discrimination

It is not illegal to harbor stereotypes and prejudices.[26] To a certain extent everyone forms stereotypes and prejudices about certain groups— both positive and negative. However, when someone *acts* on a stereotype or prejudice by excluding or harming others, discrimination has likely occurred.

The United States has had to confront various forms of discrimination throughout its history. Some forms of discrimination were regional and were based on misguided public attitudes. For example, in the mid-1800s, Irish immigrants were stereotyped as being lazy drunks. Many of these immigrants were also Roman Catholic, a religion that was considered objectionable to the predominantly Protestant American population. These stereotypes and prejudices were manifest in discrimination against the Irish immigrants. Employers during this time period advertised job openings that specifically stated, "No Irish Need Apply."

Others forms of discrimination are institutional in nature. For example, in the years following the Civil War, the new African American citizens had challenges assimilating into a predominantly white

American society. Jim Crow laws were passed, creating institutionalized segregation and discrimination. These laws mandated that whites and blacks use separate water fountains and restrooms and required whites and blacks to sit separately in restaurants, buses, and trains. There were separate schools, colleges, and libraries. Although blacks were citizens of the United States, they were denied the right to vote in some states through poll taxes, literacy tests, and intimidation. Marriages between whites and people of color were illegal in some states. Black Americans were discriminated against simply because of the color of their skin, and laws enforced this discrimination.

Over the years, minority groups have had to fight overt forms of discrimination to achieve equal status in society. Today, federal and state laws make discrimination based on such factors as race, gender, religion, and national origin illegal. These laws have greatly reduced incidents of overt discrimination. Now discrimination may be more nuanced. Some point to wage discrepancies between men and women workers hired to perform the same job. Across the board women tend to receive less compensation than men.[27] Others point to the lack of minority representation in executive posts in large companies.[28] Whether these examples are indicative of current discriminatory practices or the result of lack of past educational or employment opportunity is difficult to determine. Higher education institutions play an important role in leveling the playing field. In the context of civility, people must look beyond negative stereotypes and prejudices and treat others with dignity and respect as humans and fellow citizens.

MAKING PROGRESS

Americans continue to learn how to live in diverse communities with people of varying races, colors, ethnicities, national origins, sexual orientations, and many other characteristics. Establishing communities where *all* people are treated equally with mutual respect and dignity is essential to achieving a civil society.

While Americans have encountered challenges with diversity, we must acknowledge the significant progress that has been made. The election of Barack Obama, son of a white mother and a black father, to be president in 2008 was a significant milestone given our history of racial prejudice and discrimination.

An increase in minority enrollment in colleges and universities has brought about student populations that are becoming more representative of the population as a whole.

American citizens continue to be free to worship however they choose, without fear of retribution by the government or other religious factions; Christians, Muslims, and Jews *peacefully* coexist in communities across the country.

Homosexuals are able to start families, adopt children, and in some states marry.

People with disabilities are afforded educational opportunities and accommodations to participate more fully in society.

Learning to respect diversity in American society is not an easy task. Many groups in our communities espouse views that are diametrically opposed to each other. People have different values, beliefs, and agendas. It can be tempting to look at those who are different as being the enemy. Regardless of how different we are, however, we share the same American values and ideals. In an increasingly diverse nation, *doing civility* becomes essential, and colleges and universities are playing an integral role.

TOOLS AND EXERCISES

Diversity Test

While students may have more opportunities in college to mix with others of diverse backgrounds, more often than not they tend to find friends or interact in extracurricular social groups that consist of people from similar racial, cultural, or religious circumstances. At many small colleges, the student body may be fairly homogenous due to its religious or regional affiliations. In the end, students choose colleges, clubs, Greek organizations, and friends where they feel most comfortable. This tendency of humans to draw toward what we know and what comforts helps us to feel validated and safe. But what are we missing when we do not explore what we do not know or understand? The following exercise is intended to bring awareness to your choices regarding self-segregation. Make a list of your five to ten best friends. After you have done this, list their:

1. Race
2. Socioeconomic status
3. Religion
4. Age
5. Sexual orientation
6. Political affiliation

Diversity Challenge

As human beings, we share universal commonalities. For example, most would agree that all people, regardless of their background, share a common desire to live in a safe and secure community. Another might be that we all would like to be respected and treated as equals. Your challenge is to approach someone from a different racial, religious, or age group from yours, introduce yourself, and ask what he or she believes all people have in common.

One of the things I learned when I was
negotiating was that until I changed
myself, I could not change others.
— **Nelson Mandela**

CHAPTER 8

Civility and
the Community

To challenge rampant, pervasive incivility, we must learn how to do civility. While recognizing the problem is an important first step, the logical second step is asking, "What can we do about it?" This is a substantive and difficult question to answer. To presume that anyone could create a one-size-fits-all standard, rubric, or framework that would provide an enlightened "pathway to civility" is unrealistic. The underlying issues creating the civility dilemma in our society are too complex. They involve external cultural influences as well as complicated internal moral choices. Sometimes the lines distinguishing civility and incivility are woefully blurred. Nevertheless, certain criteria can be used to provide guideposts.

Within the context of this book, civility has been defined as encompassing two core concepts: mutual respect toward others and community engagement. Mutual respect involves treating others with the same manner of kindness, dignity, and value as you would want to receive. This concept is akin to the Golden Rule that requires people to do unto others as they would have them do unto you. Mutual respect is not just reserved for family, friends, and people who share your worldview. Mutual respect should be extended to everyone—the clerk at the grocery store, the waitress at the corner café, the homeless man walking down the street, or the politician you just cannot tolerate. Mutual respect does not mean that you must like the person, agree with the person, or suppress your disagreement or opposition to that person's views. Mutual respect *does* require you to extend respect and empathy to others. Deep disagreement between you and others does not cloud the fact that everyone has value.

Community engagement involves taking proactive steps to better the community in which you live. In a culture that tends to focus on self-indulgence, community engagement is a paradigm shift for many. The focus on community engagement requires one to look to others' needs, not as means to achieve some personal agenda but as a way of genuinely improving and strengthening the community. Meaningful community engagement may be achieved a number of ways—volunteering time to a local nonprofit organization, hospital, or school; contributing resources to a food pantry, women's shelter, church, or political organization; setting up meals for a sick friend; or talking to a new person on campus or in the apartment complex or neighborhood. The goal is *civitas*—making the community a better place for everyone.

When you attempt to do civility, the guideposts are the two prongs of the civility definition: mutual respect toward others and community engagement. When you contemplate doing civility, consider whether the act in question involves mutual respect toward others. If it does, chances are you are on solid footing with regard to civility. If it does not, reassess your motives. How would you feel if someone responded to you in the same manner you respond to him or her? Are you attempting to demean another person, or do you simply disagree with the other person's point of view? Could your conduct be misconstrued? Is there a way to adjust your response to communicate your point without escalating conflict?

Next assess the potential impact of your conduct on the community. A community can be as small as a close group of friends, campus, or workplace. It can be as large as a city, a state, or even a country. If your conduct strengthens the community, chances are it is civil. However, if the act creates schisms within the community or harms the community, even unintentionally, the conduct is likely uncivil.

The dual guideposts of mutual respect and community engagement provide a flexible working framework to assess civility and incivility. The goal of civility is not just to be a nice person. Niceness does not necessarily equal civility. The concept of civility is much deeper than a superficial display of pleasantries. In our complicated lives, conflict, discord, and bitter disagreement may be necessary. Political discussion is a perfect example of this point. Expressing genuine differences in opinions, values, and beliefs is not uncivil per se, particularly when disagreement is taken from the perspective of mutual respect and the outcome will strengthen the community.

This chapter discusses some ways that real people in our communities attempt to do civility. These innovative people seek to live in a way that respects diverse groups. They also deliberately attempt to engage in conduct that will result in tangible benefits to others in their communities. While they have not cornered the market on civility, they provide examples of ways we, too, can think differently or see ourselves in the broader contexts of our citizenship locally, nationally, and internationally. It is hoped these stories will inspire us to want to serve, help, and give.

POLICY DEVELOPMENT TO ADDRESS INCIVILITY

One response to improving civility in our schools, workplaces, and communities is to develop civility policies. Throughout the United States, administrators, employers, and elected officials have responded to the lack of civility by enacting policies, codes of conduct, and legislation to encourage greater civility. These policies run the continuum from complex and legalistic to simple and aspirational and have been met with varied results. In one example of legislation, residents of Middleborough, Massachusetts, passed an ordinance that allows the police to impose a twenty-dollar fine against individuals who use foul language in public.[1] If the police catch people using foul language, they will issue tickets.

Similarly, the NFL and thirty-two NFL teams have adopted a more legalistic official code of conduct for fans. Among other things, this code restricts conduct such as foul language, obscene gestures, intoxication, and verbal or physical harassment of an opposing team's fans.[2] Like the Middleborough ordinance, this code of conduct has some teeth. Fans who violate the code may be subject to ejection from the game and loss of ticket privileges for future games.

On the other end of the spectrum is the Washington Metropolitan Area Transit Authority, which has adopted a list of aspirational rules and manners for patrons riding the Metro. These rules do not impose fines or penalties for uncivil conduct; they suggest things Metro riders should do, such as be courteous, put trash in bins, and give your seat to someone who needs it more than you.[3]

California State University San Marcos has developed a unique policy to encourage civility on campus. The university has set up a civility committee, consisting of students, administrators, and faculty, that randomly awards gift cards and T-shirts to students they observe engaging in civil and courteous conduct on campus.[4] The civility committee operates within the institution's larger Civility Campaign that includes specific policy language on shared "community values," which are communicated to students during new student orientations for freshmen and transfer students.[5] Rather than punish a student for using foul language, being intoxicated, or making obscene gestures, the university hopes to encourage good behavior by awarding random gifts.

Admittedly, many of these ideas may appear to be superficial. Nevertheless, policy makers are truly coping with ways to promote and do civility in their communities. Will NFL spectators refrain from using foul or abusive language during games? Are Metro riders now more likely to give up their seats to pregnant women? Can the promise of a Starbucks gift card or a T-shirt truly encourage students to alter their conduct? It's hard to say. Perhaps the more important purpose behind these civility initiatives is to put the community on notice regarding expected standards of conduct.

THE POWER OF ONE

While civility policies attempt to set community-wide standards, individuals ultimately control how they choose to respond to others. All of the civility policies, programs, and initiatives in the world cannot cause people to change unless they are first willing to alter their behavior and attempt to see the world through a different lens. Sure, there are societal factors, cultural influences, and complex life experiences that shape an individual's personality, temperament, and behavior. Yet these external environmental factors do *not* define who they are.

When someone cuts us off on a highway, we choose whether to become aggressive or extend a bit more grace. When someone takes a political position that is vastly different from our own, we choose whether to criticize and attack or attempt to understand. When someone looks, speaks, or believes differently than we do, we choose whether to judge or extend dignity and respect. Each of us has the power to ultimately change the course of our relationships with our friends, family, and community by extending civility first.

Breaking the cycle of incivility takes people who are willing to choose civility when incivility is the easy default. It takes people who are willing to extend civility even when it may not be reciprocated. It takes people who can shift the focus from themselves to others. It takes people who treat others with mutual respect despite their differences. In so many circumstances, it takes just one person to buck the status quo of incivility, inspiring others to do the same. To pay it forward.

While much of this book has focused on examples of people whose conduct is less than civil, there are incredible people all around us who are doing extraordinary things. Some of these people are well-known celebrities, and others are just average people who see things differently.

All of these people share a deep-rooted mutual respect toward diverse people and a keen awareness of the needs of their community.

Star Power

While some celebrities are known for their propensity for wild parties, outlandish behavior, and lavish lifestyles, others have used their power and influence to do remarkable things. From Oprah Winfrey and George Lucas to Ryan Seacrest and Dr. Dre, some celebrities have been champions for charities and have invested heavily in causes such as educating children, empowering the disenfranchised and addressing poverty at home and around the world.[6]

In 2013, soccer superstar David Beckham signed a five-month contract to play for Paris Saint-Germain and donated his entire salary to a children's charity.[7] Irish rocker Bono has created the (RED) charity, which has raised $207 million to eradicate AIDS in Africa.[8] The charity provides life-saving drugs that prevent the transmission of AIDS from mothers to their babies.[9] The Oprah Winfrey Foundation has awarded hundreds of grants to organizations that support the education and empowerment of women, children, and families in the United States and around the world.[10] The Michael J. Fox Foundation has raised millions of dollars to fund research to cure Parkinson's disease.[11]

The Jon Bon Jovi Soul Foundation sponsors a community restaurant called the Soul Kitchen that serves healthy and delicious meals in a warm and welcoming setting in Red Bank, New Jersey.[12] The hallmark of the restaurant is that there are no prices for anything on the menu. A person can pay the suggested minimum price for the meal or, if unable to pay, can volunteer at the Soul Kitchen in lieu of payment. The concept is to provide a model that allows everyone in the community to enjoy a healthy meal and promotes volunteerism within the community.

These are just a few examples of celebrities who are making a difference at home and around the world. These famous people have been able to use their celebrity status to help others and encourage community engagement. They realize that success and fame are hollow and often fleeting. Just one person can inspire others to be a force for positive change. Amazing things can be accomplished when needs of others are acknowledged within the community.

Taking Care of Business

Corporations are also active in investing in the community through philanthropy in the communities where they operate. For example, in 2010, Kroger, the Cincinnati-based grocery chain, gave away $64 million, or 10.9 percent, of its pretax profits, and Macy's gave away 8.1 percent of profits.[13] In 2012, Target contributed 4.7 percent of its profits and pledged to donate $1 billion to public education.[14]

Highly compensated corporate CEOs have also contributed to community outreach. For example, Facebook's founder Mark Zuckerberg has pledged $100 million to help public schools in Newark, New Jersey, and has donated roughly a half billion dollars to the Silicon Valley Community Foundation.[15]

The Bill and Melinda Gates Foundation donates billions of dollars in grants every year to help communities in all fifty states and the District of Columbia and more than one hundred countries.[16] The Gates Foundation is guided by the belief that "every life has equal value," and the foundation endeavors to "help all people lead healthy, productive lives."[17] The foundation, which has in excess of $36 billion in assets, received a $30 billion pledge in 2006 from Warren Buffett, primary shareholder and CEO of Berkshire Hathaway.[18]

Andrew Carnegie, a tycoon in the steel industry, donated $350 million in his lifetime for charitable purposes. In 1905, Carnegie established a foundation to improve education in America. To this end, the Carnegie Foundation helped build nearly 1,700 libraries throughout the United States. The foundation continues to fund grants to improve education.

These highly successful American corporations and CEOs have made it a point not to focus just on profits but also to give back to their communities. They understand that their remarkable wealth and influence should not to be hoarded but used to promote good. For example, Andrew Carnegie said, "The man who dies thus rich, dies disgraced."[19]

Sometimes corporations and CEOs face scrutiny for their philanthropy, and critics question their motives. Are corporations and CEOs genuinely concerned about humanity, or is their philanthropic giving a clever marketing scheme to mask questionable business practices and gain more favorable tax treatment? These are legitimate concerns. While it is difficult, if not impossible, to know exactly the motive for making a contribution to the community, it is hard to argue with the good work that has been done with the generous contributions of corporate benefactors.

Hometown Heroes

It is not only the rich and famous who make a difference in their communities. Just ask Albert Lexie. Lexie works at the Children's Hospital of Pittsburgh as a shoeshine man. In 2012, Lexie gave the children's hospital $200,000 in tips he had collected over the last thirty years.[20] The money went toward the hospital's free care fund that helps parents who can't afford to pay their sick children's medical costs. Working at the hospital, Lexie saw firsthand the children and families the hospital served, and he wanted to do his part. Rather than keep the $200,000 for his retirement, Lexie saw a need in his community and filled it.

When Larry Swilling learned that his wife of fifty-eight years was experiencing kidney failure and needed a transplant immediately, he was concerned that she would not survive before a donor was found. So one morning he purchased the materials to make a sandwich board sign that read, "Need kidney 4 wife" along with his telephone number. Without telling his wife, Swilling began to pound the pavement in his hometown of Anderson, South Carolina. Seventy-eight years old at the time, Swilling walked 15 miles in 97-degree heat with torn cartilage in his knee. After a local news team stopped Swilling for an interview, his story went viral online. Swilling received close to two thousand calls from complete strangers willing to donate a kidney. Luckily Swilling was able to find a match, a forty-one-year-old woman from Virginia Beach, Virginia. Swilling said, "I'm amazed by the generosity of strangers."[21]

The Presidents' Pledge Against Global Poverty is a group of current and former college presidents who have publicly pledged to donate 5 percent or more of their total compensation annually to charities that fight extreme global poverty. This charity was started by Reverend Ann M. Svennungsen, former president of Texas Lutheran University.[22] Reverend Svennungsen was inspired to organize these important community leaders to make a public statement. The organization hopes that the presidents who publicly pledged at least 5 percent of their salaries will raise awareness on their campuses about the importance of giving, global citizenship, and ethical living.[23]

Giving money is not the only way to demonstrate civility. For example, in the months following the massacre at Sandy Hook Elementary School in Newtown, Connecticut, the town received an outpouring of cards, letters, and gifts from people all over the country. There were so many donations that officials had to rent a warehouse with 20,000 square feet of space to contain the gifts. There are hundreds of boxes of toys, thousands of boxes of school supplies, and more than 63,000 teddy bears. The town is taking measures to preserve the letters, cards, and artwork that were sent in response to the tragedy.[24]

One letter written by an eleven-year-old, which is representative of the thousands of letters received, read: "Dear Families: I am sorry for your loss. My grandpa died three weeks ago. I'm in foster care. When my grandpa died, I was heartbroken, so I know what you're going through. I go to First Baptist Church."[25]

This young child, who was also struggling with the pain and loss of a loved one, was able to reach out to other families and a community in grief and extend condolences in a way that was both beautiful and profound. This letter was a genuine expression that people care. Although we may not be able to make everything right or give large sums of money, the fact that someone acknowledges our hurt and pain in a time of need can contribute to the healing process.

Ivan Fernandez Anaya, a Spanish cross-country runner, demonstrated civility during an international cross-country match held in Spain by intentionally losing the race. Anaya was in second place but was able to gain an advantage and had the opportunity to surge ahead when the first-place runner, Kenyan athlete Abel Mutai, mistakenly thought he completed the race and stopped running. The crowd attempted to tell Mutai to keep running; however, the race was in Spain, and Mutai did not speak Spanish. When Anaya realized his opponent's error, he guided Mutai to the finish line and took second place.[26] When asked why he helped Mutai win the race, Anaya said, "I didn't deserve to win it. I did what I had to do. He was the rightful winner. He created a gap that I couldn't have closed if he hadn't made a mistake."[27]

Every day we make choices that affect the way we interact with others and the community. Civility requires us to look at others slightly differently. First, we must be willing to extend respect to those we encounter, particularly those who are different from us. Second, we must be willing to look beyond our own needs, to those of the community at large. Often this requires us to disconnect the ear buds, put the mobile phone on vibrate, and really look around. Are we able to see the Larry Swillings of the world, in dire straits, looking for help? Are we willing to give of ourselves to strengthen the community? Are we willing to help a neighbor, even when it might be counter to our self-interest, because it is the right thing to do? There are many ways to make a real difference and do civility.

DOING CIVILITY ON THE CAMPUS

College students can also make a significant difference in their communities. The Corporation for National and Community Service estimated that in 2011, 26.6 percent of college students nationally performed unpaid volunteer activities.[28] Tutoring and mentoring are among the most popular volunteer activities of college students.[29] Other popular options for student volunteers include fund-raising for a cause, helping a friend or neighbors following a tragedy or disaster, and participating in civic, religious, and school groups.

Colleges and universities increasingly encourage students to volunteer in their community through service learning programs. Service learning is a teaching and learning strategy that integrates relevant classroom instruction with meaningful community service.[30] Some colleges offer courses that have a required service learning component. Students must volunteer with an off-campus nonprofit to receive full credit for the course.[31] Other colleges offer grants to students and student organizations for community service projects.[32] These grants typically require students to submit a proposal and obtain a faculty sponsor and may require a final report on how the grant money was used in the community. Grants may range in amount from $100 to $3,000, depending on the proposal and the institution's budget. Several private and public grants are available for students to launch an independent service learning project.

Emma Pickering, a student at the University of Texas at Austin, wanted to use her love of painting to help children from low-income families express themselves through art.[33] She found a nonprofit organization online that made grants for student service learning projects. Pickering's proposal was accepted, and she received nearly $2,000 to use to purchase supplies for her service learning project called "Drawn for Good." Her project provided free art classes for adolescents in the Austin area.

Following the devastating tornados that hit Alabama in 2011, twenty-nine students from the University of Hartford took an "alternate spring break" to help in the ongoing disaster relief efforts.[34] The students worked closely with the Red Cross and volunteered with reconstruction efforts, including home improvements, debris removal, and planting projects. The students also volunteered at food banks, Head Start programs, and soup kitchens.

WE ARE SIMILAR IN MORE WAYS
THAN WE ARE DIFFERENT

People do civility every day. From rendering assistance to a complete stranger on the side of the road during a medical emergency to donating blood to the Red Cross, millions of acts of mutual respect, kindness, and benevolence occur every day. Yet these acts of civility are dwarfed by the clamor of incivility, which seems to get much more attention.

We all contend with incivility in multiple facets of our lives. Incivility seems to spread like a cancer and destroy our relationships with others and the cohesion that is necessary to have a vibrant and diverse community. Incivility is counterproductive and creates a hostile environment that is not conducive to learning, working, and living.

Cultural and societal forces divide us over issues, values, and beliefs. Rather than work together to achieve a common good and strengthen the community, we choose to fight over agendas and force change, based on a battle of public opinion waged in the media. However, many Americans have come to the conclusion that enough is enough. We do not need to be mired in the continued incivility that surrounds us. We can choose to go against the grain and do civility, treating others with mutual respect and dignity and engaging the community in a meaningful way that makes it a better place for everyone. This responsibility is not just for politicians, celebrities, and the elite. This is a responsibility for everyone. Each one of us can make a difference. Now is the time to do civility.

TOOLS AND EXERCISES

Get Going!

Enough reading. We can talk about civility all day, but let's see if you can put your money where your mouth is. Challenge yourself to one of the following this week:

1. Find out about alternative spring break options on campus designed to create volunteer opportunities.
2. Join or start your own Political Engagement Club that fosters respectful dialogue and solution-focused ideas across party lines.
3. Find a local organization off campus to which you could commit to volunteering once a week.
4. Register to vote, and get three other unregistered people you know to register.
5. Brainstorm with your group of friends about other ways in which you can become involved on campus and in your community.

Time Travel

One month from now, where will you be? More specifically, will you be *doing* civility? After you have completed the exercises in this book, one month from now take the Civility Index Quiz at the end of chapter 1 again. How have things changed or remained the same? What might you do differently? Is there still room for growth, or have you reached a comfortable level of civility? How does that look and feel for you? Have you noticed any changes in the way others relate to you and how you see the world?

About the Author

Kent M. Weeks draws on a wide range of experience in addressing the topic of civility on college and university campuses. He served as a college administrator, taught at The College of Wooster, and for twenty-five years taught undergraduate and graduate students in public policy and school and higher education law at George Peabody College, Vanderbilt University, where he was awarded the Peabody College Roundtable Award for excellence in teaching.

Weeks practices law in Nashville, Tennessee, where he focuses on legal and policy issues affecting higher education and observes his clients wrestling with issues arising from increasing incivility on college campuses. His writing is informed by them and by insights from his students.

He has written several books and published more than sixty articles and papers for scholarly journals and educational publications, and he currently edits *Lex Collegii*, a legal newsletter for colleges and universities. His writings focus on academic and student issues such as student civility, ethical behavior of faculty, plagiarism, and bullying. His book *A Leaner America: Private Choices and Public Policies*, examines the causes of the startling epidemic of obesity and zeros in on the efforts needed to address this problem. He recently completed *In Search of Civility: Confronting*

Incivility on the College Campus, which generated broad support and many significant comments. This is a companion book to *In Search of Civility*. Weeks also wrote a book on Adam Clayton Powell, one of the most controversial members of the U.S. House of Representatives.

Weeks consults with colleges throughout the United States and served as general counsel to Africa University in Zimbabwe for more than twenty years. His professional association recently named him as a Fellow in recognition of exceptional scholarship and service on behalf of colleges and universities.

Involved in many community activities, Weeks chaired the first elected School Board for Nashville-Davidson County and was later honored for his work in obtaining a settlement of the twenty-eight-year desegregation litigation.

A Fulbright scholar, Weeks earned a Ph.D. in political science from Case Western Reserve University, a law degree from Duke University, an M.A. from the University of New Zealand, and a B.A. from The College of Wooster in Ohio.

Bibliography

Carter, Stephen L. *Civility: Manners, Morals, and the Etiquette of Democracy* (New York: Basic, 1998). Addresses a general audience.

Dahnke, Cassandra, and Tomas Spath,. *Reclaiming Civility in the Public Square: 10 Rules that Work* (Livermore, CA: WingSpan Press, 2007). Addresses the needs to improve relationships in public and governmental areas.

Davis, James Calvin. *In Defense of Civility* (Louisville, KY: Westminster John Knox Press, 2010). Examines the role of religion in public moral debate, past and present.

Forni, P. M. *The Civility Solution: What to Do When People Are Rude* (New York: St. Martin's Press, 2008). Includes a general discussion of civility in personal behavior.

Guinness, Os. *The Case for Civility* (New York: HarperCollins, 2008). Examines Civility in America and is a proposal on how to achieve this goal.

Herbst, Susan. *Rude Democracy* (Philadelphia: Temple University Press, 2010).Examines contemporary American political culture.

Kidder, Rushworth M. *Shared Values for a Troubled World* (San Francisco: Jossey-Bass, 1994). Searches for a global code of ethics.

Richardson, Steven M., ed. *Promoting Civility: A Teaching Challenge* (San Francisco: Jossey-Bass, 1999). Examines the issues related to civility and classroom teaching.

Twale, Darla J. *Faculty Incivility* (San Francisco: Jossey-Bass, 2008). Reviews incivility in today's world and includes personal stories of faculty victims.

Weeks, Kent M. *In Search of Civility* (New York: Morgan James Publishing, 2011). Provides a higher education context for understanding civility by incorporating real-life student stories.

Williams, Redford, and Virginia Williams. *In Control: No More Snapping at Your Family, Sulking at Work . . .* (Emmaus, PA: Rodale, 2006). Studies the developments in the field of behavioral medicine and anger and control.

End Notes

Chapter 1

1   Weber Shandwick, "Civility in America 2012," http://www.webershandwick.com.

2   *Merriam-Webster Dictionary*, 11th ed., s.v. "civility."

3   P. M. Forni, *The Civility Solution: What to Do When People Are Rude* (New York: St. Martin's Press, 2008).

4   Stephen L. Carter, *Civility: Manners, Morals, and the Etiquette of Democracy* (New York: Basic, 1998).

5   Institute for Civility in Government, "What is Civility?" http://www.instituteforcivility.org/who-we-are/what-is-civility.

6   Id.

7   The National Institute for Civil Discourse, 2012, the University of Arizona, http://nicd.arizona.edu/.

8   Matthew 22:39, Revised Standard Version of the Bible.

9   Random House *Webster's Unabridged Dictionary* (2001), s.v. "civility."

10   Athenian Ephebic Oath, trans. Clarence A. Forbes, in Fletcher Harper Swift, *The Athenian Ephebic Oath of Allegiance in American Schools and Colleges* (Los Angeles: University of California Press, 1947), 4.

11   The E Pluribus Unum Project, Assumption College, "America in the 1770s, 1850s, and 1920s," http://www1.assumption.edu/ahc/.

12   E. Fletcher, "Stung by Sacha Baron Cohen: Borat's Etiquette Consultant," *Daily Telegraph,* June 25, 2009.

13   Entertainment Software Rating Board, Rating Guide, http://www.esrb.org/ratings/ratings_guide.jsp.

14   Devin Kelly, "After Sandy Hook School Starts the Year with Heightened Security," *Los Angeles Times,* August 11, 2013.

15   *Forni, supra note 3, at 48–53.*

16   *Id.*

17   Kent M. Weeks and Ernie E. Gilkes, "Higher Education Confronts the Workplace Bully," *Lex Collegii* 36 (Winter 2013).

18   The Salt March, The History Channel, http://www.history.com/topics/salt-march.

19   The Henry Ford, "The Story Behind the Bus," 2002, www.thehenryford.org.

20   Sheridan Harvey, "Marching for the Vote: Remembering the Woman Suffrage Parade of 1913," Library of Congress, memory.loc.gov.

21   Rushworth M. Kidder, *Shared Values for a Troubled World* (San Francisco: Jossey-Bass, 1994).

Chapter 2

1   Pew Research Center for the People and the Press, "Partisan Polarization Surges in Bush, Obama Years, Trends in American Values: 1987–2012," June 4, 2012, http://www.people-press.org.

2   Weber Shandwick, "Civility in America 2012," http://www.webershandwick.com.

3   The National Institute for Civil Discourse, 2012, the University of Arizona, http://nicd.arizona.edu/.

4   Susan Herbst, *Rude Democracy* (Philadelphia: Temple University Press, 2010).

5   Deborah Caldwell, "Eleven Historic Fights Worse than the Sequester," March 12, 2013, CNBC.com.

6   Jim Toedtman, "Leaders, Try Greatness, Not Meanness," *AARP,* July 2, 2012.

7   Caldwell, *supra* note 5.

8   Id.

9   Cornell W. Clayton, "Civility Crisis of Politics Is Just a Symptom of Division," *Seattle Times,* October 27, 2012.

10 Robert McNamara, "The Election of 1828 Was Marked by Dirty Tactics," About.com.

11 Caldwell, *supra* note 5.

12 "The Kansas-Nebraska Act of 1854," National Archives, http://www.archives.gov.

13 Audie Cornish, "Segregation Forever: A Fiery Pledge Forgiven, But Not Forgotten," National Public Radio (NPR), January 10, 2013.

14 Id.

15 Timeline: Civil Rights Era (1954–1971), PBS, http://www.pbs.org.

16 Vietnam War Protests, The History Channel, http://www.history.com.

17 Gary Tuchman, "Kent State Forever Linked with Vietnam War Era," CNN.com, May 4, 2000.

18 Ben Smith, "Source: Wilson Breaks $1 Million," Politico, September 12, 2009, http:www.politico.com.

19 Herbst, *supra* note 4.

20 Id.

21 Bryan T. Gervais, "The Effects of Incivility in News Media on Political Deliberation: The Mimicry of Uncivil Language in Political Opinions," prepared for presentation at the American Politics Workshop, University of Maryland, March 18, 2011.

22   Pew Research Center, "Millennials: Confident. Connected. Open
     to Change," February 2010, http://www.pewsocialtrends.org/
     files/2010/10/millennials-confident-connected-open-to-change.
     pdf.

23   Id.

24   Id.

25   Id.

26   Id.

27   Id.

28   Regina Conley, "Young Voter Turnout Increases from 2008 to
     2012," November 8, 2012, http://redalertpolitics.com.

29   Tyler Kingkade, "Youth Vote 2012 Turnout: Exit Polls Show
     Greater Share of Electorate Than in 2008," *Huffington Post*,
     November 7, 2012.

30   Id.

31   Abby Kiesa, Alexander P. Orlowski, Peter Levine, et al.,
     "Millennials Talk Politics: A Study of College Student Political
     Engagement," The Center for Information and Research on Civic
     Learning and Engagement, Tufts University November 2006,
     http://www.civicyouth.org/college-students-talk-politics.

32   Id.

33   Id.

34   Suzanne Pritzker, Melanie J. Springer, and Amanda M. McBride,
     "Learning to Vote: Informing Political Participation Among
     College Students," Center for Social Development, Washington
     University in St. Louis, 2012.

35   Massachusetts Historical Society, "The Boston Tea Party," http://
     www.masshist.org/revolution/teaparty.php.

36   BBC, "An Archive of World War II Memories," March 2012,
     http://www.bbc.co.uk/history/ww2peopleswar/timeline/factfiles/
     nonflash/a6652262.shtml.

37   United States Courts, "First Amendment: Free Speech and Flag
     Burning," http://www.uscourts.gov/educational-resources/get-

involved/constitution-activities/first-amendment/free-speech-flag-burning.aspx.

38   Madison Gray, "The L.A. Riots: 15 Years After Rodney King," *Time*, 2007, http://content.time.com/time/specials/2007/la_riot/article/0,28804,1614117_1614084_1614831,00.html.

39   BBC, "1997: Princes Diana Died in Paris Crash," http://news.bbc.co.uk/onthisday/hi/dates/stories/august/31/newsid_2510000/2510615.stm.

Chapter 3

1   Kaiser Family Foundation, "Generation M2: Media in the Lives of 8- to 18-year olds," January 2010, http://kaiserfamilyfoundation.files.wordpress.com/2013/04/8010.pdf.

2   Bureau of Labor Statistics, "American Time Use Survey," June 22, 2012, www.bls.gov/news.release/atus.nr0.htm.

3   David Hinckley, "Americans Spend 34 Hours a Week Watching Television According to Nielsen Numbers," *New York Daily News*, September 19, 2012, http://www.nydailynews.com/entertainment/tv-movies/americans-spend-34-hours-week-watching-tv-nielsen-numbers-article-1.1162285.

4   Id.

5   Sasha Emmons, "Is Media Violence Damaging to Kids?" CNN.com, February 21, 2013, http://www.cnn.com/2013/02/21/living/parenting-kids-violence-media.

6   RAND Health, "Does Watching Sex on Television Influence Teens' Sexual Activity?" 2004, http://www.rand.org/pubs/research_briefs/RB9068/index1.html.

7   Daniel M. Shea, and Barbara Steadman, "Nastiness, Name-Calling and Negativity, The Allegheny College Survey of Civility and Compromise in American Politics," Allegheny College, http://sitesmedia.s3.amazonaws.com/civility/files/2010/04/AlleghenyCollegeCivilityReport2010.pdf.

8   American Bar Association, "Civility and Free Expression in
     Popular Culture," 2013, http://www.americanbar.org/groups/
     public_education/initiatives_awards/civility/civility_and_
     freeexpressioninpopularculture.html.

9   Weber Shandwick, *supra* note 2.

10   RAND Health, *supra* note 6.

11   Rebecca L. Collins, Steven C. Martino, and Rebecca Shaw,
     "Influence of Media on Adolescent Sexual Health: Evidence and
     Opportunities," Office of the Assistant Secretary for Planning and
     Evaluation, U.S. Department of Health and Human Services,
     April 2011, http://aspe.hhs.gov .

12   Jennifer Peltz, "Brett Favre Sexting Suit Settled in NYC,"
     Associated Press, May 24, 2013; Jonathan Lemire and Jennifer
     Peltz, "Weiner Faces Growing Calls to Quit Mayor's Race,"
     Associated Press, July 25, 2013.

13   Jason Carroll, Laura Padilla-Walker, Larry Nelson, et. al.,
     "Generation XXX: Pornography Acceptance and Use Among
     Emerging Adults," *Journal of Adolescent Research* 23 (January
     2008): 6-30.

14   Matthew Balan, "CNN Highlights Pornography's Destructive
     Effect on Society?" NewsBusters.org, July 28, 2010, http://
     newsbusters.org/blogs/matthew-balan/2010/07/28/cnn-highlights-
     pornographys-destructive-effects-society.

15   Id.

16   John D. Foubert, Matthew W. Brosi, and Sean Bannon,
     "Pornography Viewing Among Fraternity Men: Effects on
     Bystander Intervention, Rape Myth Acceptance, and Behavioral
     Intent to Commit Sexual Assault," *Journal of Sexual Addiction and
     Compulsivity* 18 (2011): 212–231.

17   "Teen Pregnancy," Centers for Disease Control and Prevention,
     May 20, 2013, http://www.cdc.gov/teenpregnancy.

18   "Sexually Transmitted Diseases Surveillance2011," Centers for
     Diseases Control and Prevention, December 2012, http://www.
     cdc.gov/std/stats11/Surv2011.pdf.

19 "Sandy Hook Shootings: What Happened?" CNN.com, http://www.cnn.com/interactive/2012/12/us/sandy-hook-timeline/index.html.

20 Travis Korte, "Violent Video Games, Blamed for Promoting Violence, May Benefit the Brain," *Huffington Post*, January 16, 2013.

21 Ali Russlynn, "Dear Colleague Letter: Sexual Violence Background, Summary, and Fast Facts," United States Department of Education, Office for Civil Rights, April 4, 2011, http://www.ncherm.org/documents/OCRDearColleagueLetter4.4.11.pdf.

22 L. Rowell Huesmann, Jessica Moise-Titus, Cheryl-Lynn Podolski, and Leonard D. Eron, "Longitudinal Relations Between Children's Exposure to TV Violence and Their Aggressive and Violent Behavior in Young Adulthood: 1977-1992," *Developmental Psychology* 39 2003: 201-221.

23 Eugene V. Beresin, "The Impact of Media Violence on Children and Adolescents: Opportunities for Clinical Interventions," *American Academy of Child & Adolescent Psychiatry*, 2010, www.aacap.org.

24 Huesmann, *supra* note 22.

25 Petra Rattue, "How Does Violence in the Media Impact School Bullying?" *Medical News Today*, July 18, 2012, http://www.medicalnewstoday.com/articles/247996.php.

26 Id.

27 Brad J. Bushman, and L. Rowell Huesmann, "Short-term and Long-term Effects of Violent Media on Aggression in Children and Adults," *Arch Pediatric Adolescence Medicine* 160 (April 3, 2006): 348.

28 Rick Nauert, "Negative Effects of Violent Video Games May Build Over Time," Psych Central December 11, 2012, http://psychcentral.com/news/2012/12/11/negative-effects-of-violent-video-games-may-build-over-time/48918.htm.

29 Claire Suddith, "A Brief History of Political Profanity," *Time*, June 9, 2010.

30 Adam Rose, "Dick Cheney: Telling Patrick Leahy 'F--k Yourself' Was 'Sort Of the Best Thing I Ever Did,'" *Huffington Post*, June 23, 2010.

31 Bianca Bosker, "Yahoo CEO Carol Bartz to Michael Arrington: 'F**k Off,'" *Huffington Post*, May 24, 2010.

32 Urban Dictionary, s.v. "Casual Profanity."

Chapter 4

1 Lauren Pac, "2 Ex-Students Accused of Altering Grades," *Dayton Daily News*, March 26, 2013, http://www.daytondailynews.com/news/news/former-miami-students-face-criminal-charges-allege/nW39t.

2 "Former Miami University Student Pleads Guilty to Hacking Computer," ABC Channel 9, Cincinnati, April 26, 2013.

3 Id.

4 Jenny Anderson, "SAT and ACT to Tighten Rules after Cheating Scandal," *New York Times*, March 27, 2012.

5 "Cheating in College Is Widespread—But Why?" Talk of the Nation, NPR, July 19, 2010.

6 Id.

7 David Callahan, "On Campus: Author Discusses the 'Cheating Culture' with College Students," *Plagiary* 1, no. 4 (2006): 1–8.

8 Donna Stuber-McEwen, Phillip Wiseley, and Susan Hoggatt, "Point, Click, and Cheat: Frequency and Type of Academic Dishonesty in the Virtual Classroom," *Online Journal of Distance Learning and Administration* 7, no. 3 (Fall 2009).

9 Kent M. Weeks, "Academic Dishonesty," *Lex Collegii* 30, no. 4 (Spring 2007).

10 Jeffrey R. Young, "High-tech Cheating on Homework Abounds, and Professors Bear Some Blame," *Chronicle of Higher Education*, March 28, 2010.

11 Amy Novotney, "Beat the Cheat," *Monitor on Psychology* 42, no. 6 (June 2011), http://www.apa.org/monitor/2011/06/cheat.aspx.

12 Eric A. Storch, and Jason B. Storch, "Academic Dishonesty and Attitudes Towards Academic Dishonest Acts: Support for Cognitive Dissonance Theory," *Psychological Reports* 92 (2003): 174–177.

13 Russell K. Baker, Priscilla Berry, and Barry Thornton, "Student Attitudes on Academic Integrity Violations," *Journal of College Teaching & Learning* 5 (2008): 5–13.

14 Novotney, *supra* note 11.

15 *Black's Law Dictionary*, 6th ed.

16 Dan Berrett, "Harvard Cheating Scandal Points Out the Ambiguities of Collaboration," *Chronicle of Higher Education*, September 5, 2012.

17 Katherine Landergan, "Half of Students in Harvard Cheating Scandal Required to Withdraw from the College." Boston.com, February 1, 2013.

18 Luke Winn, "Harvard to Be without Casey, Curry in Wake of Cheating Scandal," *Sports Illustrated*, September 11, 2012.

19 Hermann Maurer, Frank Kappe, and Bilal Zaka, "Plagiarism—A Survey," *Journal of Universal Computer Science* 12, no 8 (2006). Also see NPR *supra* note 5.

20 Id.

21 Maurer, *supra* note 19.

22 Weeks, *supra* note 9.

23 Stuber-McEwen, *supra* note 8.

24 Cora M. Dzubak, "Classroom Decorum: What's Happening and Does it Matter?" The Association for the Tutoring Profession, 2012, http://www.myatp.org/wp-content/uploads/2012/06/Synergy-Vol-2-Dzubak-Chaos.pdf.

25 Wendy L. Bjorklund and Diana L. Rehling, "Student Perceptions of Classroom Incivility," *College Teaching* 58 (2010): 15-18.

26 Dzubak, *supra* note 24.

27 Id.

28 Bjorklund and Rehling, *supra* note 25.

29 Id.

30 Lloyd J. Feldman, "Classroom Civility Is Another of Our Instructor Responsibilities," *College Teaching* 49 (2001): 137-140.

31 Bjorklund and Rehling, *supra* note 25.

32 Middle Tennessee State University, Learning Teaching & Innovative Technology Center, "Tips for Dealing with Uncivil Behavior in Large Classes," http://www.mtsu.edu/ltanditc/docs/tips_for_Dealing_with_uncivil_behavior_in_large_classes.pdf.

33 Schroeder, Jennifer L. and Robertson, H., "Civility in the College Classroom," *Association for Psychological Science* (November 2008).

34 Bjorklund and Rehling, *supra* note 25.

35 Jeffrey R. Young, "Sssshh. We're Taking Notes Here," *Chronicle of Higher Education*, August 8, 2003.

36 Id.

37 "Disgruntled Student Sues over C-Plus, Demands Higher Grade and $1.3 Million Damages Payout," CBSNews.com, February 13, 2013.

38 Leslie Small, "Police: Student Threatened Professors after Receiving B-," *Collegian,* May 13, 2008.

39 Id.

40 Scott Jaschick, "Knifed Over a Grade," *Inside Higher Education,* December 28, 2005.

41 Id.

42 Kaustuv Basu, "Class Problem," *Inside Higher Education,* March 26, 2012.

43 Id.

Chapter 5

1 Weeks, Kent M. "Collegiality and the Quarrelsome Professor," 20 *Lex Collegii* 1 (Summer 1996).

2 Id.

3   American Association of University Professors, *Policy Documents and Reports,* 9th ed. (Washington, D.C.: AAUP, 2001).

4   Id.

5   *Sweezy v. State of New Hampshire*, 77 S.Ct. 1203 (1957).

6   Kent M. Weeks, "The Classroom and Academic Freedom," *Lex Collegii* 30, no. 1 (Summer 2006).

7   Cary Nelson, "Defining Academic Freedom," *Inside Higher Ed,* December 21, 2010.

8   American Association of University Professors, *supra* note 3.

9   American Association of University Professors, "Freedom in the Classroom," Reports and Publications, June 2007, http://www.aaup.org/report/freedom-classroom.

10   Id.

11   American Council on Education, "Statement on Academic Rights and Responsibilities," June 23, 2005, http://www.chea.org/pdf/ACE__Statement_on_Academic_Rights_and_Responsibilities_%286_23_2005%29.pdf.

12   Id.

13   Daniele Fanelli, "How Many Scientists Fabricate and Falsify Research? A Systematic Review and Meta-Analysis of Survey Data," *PLoS ONE* 4, no. 5 (2009): e5738.

14   Id.

15   Jeffrey Brainard, "Science Fraud at Universities Is Common—and Commonly Ignored," *Chronicle of Higher Education,* June 19, 2008.

16   Id.

17   Dan Vergano, "Experts Claim 2006 Climate Report Plagiarized," *USA Today,* November 22, 2010.

18   Id.

19   National Institutes of Health, "Grantee Misconduct: Dr. Eric T. Poehlman," Press Release, March 7, 2011.

20   Elizabeth Mehren, "Prof. Ellis' Course Is Yanked Over Lies," *Los Angeles Times*, June 21, 2001.

21   Richard Monastersky, "U. of Colorado President Recommends Dismissal of Ward Churchill," *Chronicle of Higher Education,* June 8, 2007.

22   Philip J. Langlais, "Ethics for the Next Generation," *Chronicle of Higher Education,* January 13, 2006.

23   Katherine Mangan, "Service Learning Becomes the New Standard at Tulane U.," *Chronicle of Higher Education* February 21, 2010.

24   Amihai Glazer, "Op-ed: UC Irvine Faculty Call for Civility During Wall Week," *New University*, May 12, 2010.

Chapter 6

1   Ray B. Williams, "The Silent Epidemic: Workplace Bullying," Psychology Today, May 3, 2011.

2   Id.

3   AARP, "What Are the Costs of Employee Turnover?" April 14, 2011, http://www.aarp.org/work/employee-benefits/info-04-2011/what-are-the-costs-associated-with-employee-turnover.html.

4   Kent M. Weeks, and Ernie E. Gilkes, "Higher Education Confronts the Workplace Bully," *Lex Collegii* 36, no. 3 (Fall 2012).

5   Darby Dickerson, "Cyberbullies on Campus," *University of Toledo Law Review* 37, no. 1 (2005).

6   Kathleen Hart, "Sticks and Stones and Shotguns at Schools: The Ineffectiveness of Constitutional Antibullying Legislation as a Response to School Violence," *Georgia Law Review* 39 (Spring 2005): 1109.

7   Indiana State University, "Bullying Still Occurs In College, Professor Finds," Press Release, October 20, 2011, http://www.indstate.edu/news/news.php?newsid=2904.

8   Dickerson, *supra* note 5.

9   Paul R. Smokowski and Kelly Holland Kopasz, "Bullying in School: An Overview of Types, Effects, Family Characteristics, and

Intervention Strategies, *Children and Schools* 27, no. 101 (April 2005).

10 Peter Thunfors and Dewey Cornell, "The Popularity of Middle School Bullies," *Journal of School Violence* 7, no. 1 (2008): 65-82.

11 Dickerson, *supra* note 5.

12 Healthy Workplace Bill, "What is Workplace Bullying," 2013, http://www.healthyworkplacebill.org/problem.php#problem.

13 Indiana State University, *supra* note 7.

14 Bullying Statistics, "Bullying Victims," 2009, http://www.bullyingstatistics.org/content/bullying-victims.html.

15 Radha Chitale,"When Workplace Bullying Goes Too Far," ABCNew.com, March 10, 2008.

16 Dickerson, *supra* note 5.

17 Douglas E. Abrams, "Recognizing the Public Schools' Authority to Discipline Students' Off-Campus Cyberbullying of Classmates," *New England Journal on Criminal and Civil Confinement* 37, no. 181 (Summer 2011).

18 Bullying Statistics, "Bullycide," 2009, http://www.bullyingstatistics.org/content/bullycide.html.

19 Dickerson, *supra* note 5.

20 Janice Harper, "Beyond Bullying: Peace Building at Work, School, and Home," *Psychology Today*, March 28, 2013.

21 Christine Jarvis, "Workplace Bullying—The Triad: Bullies, Victims, and Bystanders," Workplace Bullying Institute, October 4, 2011, http://www.workplacebullying.org/2011/10/05/workplace-bullying-the-triad-bullies-victims-and-bystanders.

22 Jaime Lester, *Workplace Bullying in Higher Education* (New York: Routledge 2013).

23 Id.

24 Indiana State University, *supra* note 7.

25 Id.

26 Hazing Definitions, HazingPrevention.org.

27 Elizabeth J. Allan, "Hazing and the Making of Men," StopHazing.org, 2010, http://www.stophazing.org/makingofmen.htm.

28   Elizabeth J. Allan and Mary Madden, "Hazing in View: College Students at Risk," University of Maine, March 11, 2008, http://www.umaine.edu/hazingstudy/hazinginview6.htm.

29   Sara Lipka, "Student-affairs Meeting: Hazing Extends Beyond Fraternities: What Parents Expect," *Chronicle of Higher Education*, March 21, 2008.

30   HazingPrevention.org, "Hazing Information," 2011, http://www.hazingprevention.org/hazing-information.html.

31   Kyle Hightower, "Robert Champion Death: Manslaughter Added to Hazing Charges for FAMU Band Members," *Huffington Post*, March 5, 2013.

32   "After Hazing Death of Member, FAMU Marching Band Playing Again After Suspension," *Associated Press*, September 1, 2013.

33   Id.

34   Hayes Hickman, "Butt-Chugging Denied: Alexander P. Broughton, UT Student Claims He Did Not Have an Alcohol Enema" News Channel Five, Knoxville, October 3, 2012.

35   Id.

36   "Last UT Students in Butt-Chugging Case Go to Court," Local 8 Now.com, February 8, 2013.

37   Canadian Press, "No Punishment After Apparent Hazing Ritual at Ryerson." CBC News, March 25, 2013.

38   "Engineering Department Hazing at Ryerson University," YouTube, March 23, 2013.

39   "Ryerson Engineering Hazing Video," *Huffington Post Canada*, March 24, 2013, http://www.huffingtonpost.ca/2013/03/24/ryerson-engineering-hazing-video_n_2944576.html.

40   Allen and Madden, *supra* note 28.

41   Amanda Lenhart, "Cyberbullying and Online Teens," Pew Internet and American Life Project, June 27, 2007, http://www.pewinternet.org/~/media//Files/Reports/2007/PIP%20Cyberbullying%20Memo.pdf.pdf.

42   West Virginia University, Eberly College of Arts and Sciences, "WVU Researchers Look at Cyberbullying Victimization Among College Students," Press Release, March 31, 2011.

43   "College Student Sentenced in Weld County Sexting Case," ABC News, Denver, December 4, 2009, http://www.thedenverchannel. com/news/college-student-sentenced-in-weld-county-sexting-case.

44   Id.

45   Jamison Barr and Emmy Lugus, "Digital Threats on Campus: Examining the Duty of Colleges to Protect Their Social Networking Students" *Western New England Law Review*, 33, no. 757 (2011).

46   Workplace Bullying Institute, "Morrissey Family Sues University of Virginia for 2010 Suicide," August 1, 2012.

47   David McNair, "Final Days: Emails Show VQR's 'Awkward Workplace Scenario,'" *The Hook,* January 20, 2012.

48   Id.

49   Id.

50   David McNair, "Closing Chapter: VQR's Genoways Resigns, Waldo Celebrates," *The Hook,* April 4, 2012.

51   Id.

52   Laura Rowley, "The Financial Toll of Workplace Bullies," Workplace Bullying Institute, May 5, 2011, http://www. workplacebullying.org/2011/05/06/yahoo.

53   M. S.Hershcovis, "Bullying More Harmful than Sexual Harassment on the Job, Say Researchers," American Psychological Association, March 8, 2008, http://www.apa.org/news/press/ releases/2008/03/bullying.aspx.

54   Gary Namie, "U.S. Hostile Workplace Survey," Workplace Bullying Institute, 2000, http://www.workplacebullying.org/multi/ pdf/N-N-2000.pdf.

55   Id.

56   AARP, *supra* note 3.

57   CNN Money, "100 Best Companies to Work For," February 4, 2013.

58   "Diversity and Inclusion in Our Culture," Google.com.

59   Id.

60   CNN Money, *supra* note 57.

61   Id.

62   Id.

63   Susan Adams, "The Top Companies to Work for in America," *Forbes*, January 21, 2013.

Chapter 7

1   Hope Yen, "New Signs of Rising Illegal Immigration Into the US," ABCnews.com, September 23, 2013, http://abcnews.go.com/Politics/wireStory/signs-rising-illegal-immigration-us-20345380; William Booth, "One Nation, Indivisible: Is it History?" Washington Post February 22, 1998.

2   Page, Scott E. (2007). "Diversity Powers Innovation." Center for American Progress.

3   Irvin Wladowsky-Berger, "Innovation and Diversity," *Innovation America*, October-November 2006.

4   Patricia Gurin, William Bowen, et al. "The Compelling Need for Diversity in Higher Education," University of Michigan, January 1999, Expert reports prepared from *Gratz et al. v. Bollinger, et al.* No. 97-75231 (E.D. Mich.) and *Grutter, et al. v. Bollinger, et al.* No. 97-75928 (E.D. Mich.).

5   *Regents of the University of California v. Bakke*, 98 S.Ct. 2733 (1978).

6   *Grutter v. Bollinger*, 123 S.Ct. 2325 (2003).

7   Id.

8   *Fisher v. University of Texas at Austin*, 133 S. Ct. 2411 (2013).

9   Id.

10   Allie Grasgreen, "Ghosts of Hate Crimes Past," *Inside Higher Education*, March 8, 2013, www.insidehighered.com.

11   Id.

12 Thomas Graning, "Racial Slurs Yelled at Ole Miss Obama Protest," CBSnews.com, November 7, 2012.

13 Brittany Bailey, "UT Chancellor Jimmy Creek Looks into Racial Incidents on Campus," News Channel 10, Knoxville, March 26, 2010, www.wbir.com.

14 "Education: Higher Education: Institutions and Enrollment," United States Census Bureau, June 27, 2012.

15 "2010 Census Shows America's Diversity," United States Census Bureau, March 24, 2011.

16 Pew Research Religion and Public Life Project, "Religious Landscape Survey," February 2008, http://religions.pewforum.org/pdf/report-religious-landscape-study-full.pdf.

17 "Stereotypes, Prejudice and Discrimination," Connexions, July 29, 2013.

18 Henri Tajfel, *Human Groups and Social Categories: Studies in Social Psychology* (Cambridge, UK: Cambridge University Press, 1981).

19 Michael Billig, "Prejudice, Categorization, and Particularization: From a Perceptual to a Rhetorical Approach." *European Journal of Social Psychology* 15, no. 1 (1985): 79-103.

20 Gordon W. Allport, *The Nature of Prejudice* (Reading, MA: Addison-Wesley, 1954).

21 Mir Rabiul Islam, and Miles Hewstone, "Dimensions of Contact as Predictors of Intergroup Anxiety, Perceived Out-Group Variability, and Out-Group Attitude: An Integrative Model," *Personality and Social Psychology Bulletin,* 19, no. 6 (1993): 700-710.

22 Robert M. Entman and Andrew Rojecki, *The Black Image in the White Mind: Media and Race in America.* (Chicago, IL: University of Chicago Press, 2000).

23 Melissa Burkley, "Pop and Prejudice: How Modern Prejudice Is Depicted in our Pop Culture," *Psychology Today,* September 25, 2009.

24 Id.

25   Beth Potier, "Prejudice Is Not Just Black and White," *Harvard University Gazette*, April 18, 2002, http://news.harvard.edu/gazette/2002/04.18/03-banaji.html.

26   Jamie Chamberlin, "What's behind Prejudice," *American Psychology Association* 35, No. 9 (2004).

27   Sarah Jane Glynn and Audrey Powers, "The Top 10 Facts About the Wage Gap: Women Are Still Earning Less than Men Across the Board," Center for American Progress, April 16, 2012.

28   Kevin Whitelaw, "Diversity Efforts Uneven In U.S. Companies," NPR, January 11, 2010.

Chapter 8

1   Josh Sanburn, "What the @!#$? Cursing in the Public in This Massachusetts Town Will Cost You $20," *Time Business & Money*, June 13, 2012.

2   "NFL Implements Fan Code of Conduct," NFL.com, July 26, 2012, http://www.nfl.com/news/story/09000d5d809c28f9/article/nfl-teams-implement-fan-code-of-conduct.

3   Washington Metropolitan Area Transit Authority, "Metrorail Rules and Manners," 2013, http://www.wmata.com/rail/railrules.cfm.

4   Gary Warth, "CSUSM Launches Civility Campaign to Improve Campus Environment," *New York Times*, August 11, 2011.

5   Id.

6   Dresden Shumaker, "Hollywood Reporter Reveals Biggest Celebrity Philanthropists," *Babble*, July 27, 2013.

7   "David Beckham Joins PSG, Will Donate Salary to Charity," *USA Today*, January 31, 2013.

8   Randall Lane, "Bill Gates and Bono: 'Partners In Crime' Discuss Their Collaboration For Good." *Forbes*, June 6, 2013.

9   Red, "How Red Works," 2012, Joinred.com.

10   "Oprah Winfrey's Official Biography," Oprah.com, May 17, 2011.

11   Michael J Fox Foundation for Parkinson's Research, 2013, MichaelJFox.org.

12   Jon Bon Jovi Soul Kitchen, "About," 2013, Jbjsoulkitchen.org.

13   Ken Stern, "Why Corporations Give to Charity," *Slate*, August 8, 2013.

14   Id.

15   Doug Gross, "Facebook's Zuckerberg Is Nation's No. 2 Charitable Donor," CNN, February 12, 2013.

16   Id.

17   Bill and Melinda Gates Foundation, "Who We Are," gatesfoundation.org.

18   Bill and Melinda Gates Foundation, "History," gatesfoundation. org.

19   Susan Stanberg, "How Andrew Carnegie Turned His Fortune into a Library Legacy," NPR, August 1, 2013.

20   Byron Pitts, "Reporter's Notebook: Shoeshiner Donates $200K in Tips to Kids' Hospital," ABC News, June 13, 2013.

21   Elise Sole, "Man Who Walked Miles with 'Need Kidney 4 Wife' Sign Finds a Donor," Yahoo Shine Healthy Living, September 6, 2013, shine.yahoo.com/healthy-living.

22   The Presidents' Pledge Against Global Poverty, "About the Pledge," presidentspledge.org.

23   Id.

24   Diane Orson, "What Will Happen to All the Letters People Sent to Newtown?" *Morning Edition,* NPR, February 25, 2013.

25   Id.

26   "Ivan Fernandez Anaya, Spanish Runner, Intentionally Loses Race so Opponent Can Win," *Huffington Post,* January 18, 2013, http://www.huffingtonpost.com/2013/01/18/ivan-fernandez-anaya-hone_n_2505360.html.

27   Id.

28   Corporation for National and Community Service, "Volunteering and Civic Life in America," 2011, www.nationalservice.gov.

29   Corporation for National and Community Service, "College Students Helping America," October 2006, www.nationalservice.gov.

30   American Association of Community Colleges, "Service Learning," http://www.aacc.nche.edu.

31   Lasell College, "Service-Learning Linked Credit," http://www.lasell.edu/academics/academic-centers/center-for-community-based-learning/service-learning/linked-credit.html.

32   Purdue University, "Service-Learning," http://www.purdue.edue/servicelearning/Students/funding.html.

33   Beckie Supiano, "Grant Program Lets Students Take Charge of 'Service Learning'," *Chronicle of Higher Education*, March 7, 2008.

34   Katrina Rossos, "Spring Break in Alabama? Manalapan College Students Help with Tornado Recovery," *Manalapan Patch*, April 1, 2012.

CPSIA information can be obtained at www.ICGtesting.com
Printed in the USA
LVOW06s0306230414

382738LV00002B/2/P